Hooking Up
Sex and Paid Love

Zoe Déval
a memoir

IngramSpark • La Vergne, TN • Melbourne, AU

Hooking Up. Sex and Paid Love

Copyright @ 2023 Zoe Déval. All rights reserved internationally.

First published in America and Australia in 2023 by *IngramSpark*. The author, Zoe Déval asserts all her rights under international conventions, Copyright Acts and Patents Law to be rewarded as the author of this book. Names have been changed to respect privacy and anonymity.

ISBN 978-1-7386288-0-3

Book design and typesetting by supporters of Zoe Déval
in Avenir 8-10 pt on a MacBook Air.

Cover image: Royalty free stock image "Man flirting with prostitute," ID 44987139 © Katarzyna Bialasiewicz, *Dreamstime.com*.

Other chapter images copyright free, reworked graphically by the author ©. Original stock photos ©: Chapter 1. Alp Ar Tunga Jabbarli; 2. Marina Ryazantseva; 3. Михаил Шнейдер; 4., 9., 10., 13. Alexander Krivitskiy; 5. Yogendra Singh; 6. *Pixabay*; 7. *Ottonbro Studio;* 8. The Author; 11. Tainá Bernard; 12. Ricardo Garcia; 14. Sabel Blanco; Epilogue Frans van Heerden.

I'd like to acknowledge and dedicate this book
to all sex workers worldwide, especially all those
who have lost their lives through prostitution.
For their bravery, their compassion, their grit, and sheer determination
to turn their lives around, striving for freedom and independence. You
have my admiration and this is also their story.

*"It's not brothels that break up relationships.
It's affairs. Brothels often save marriages."*

~ Zoe Déval.

*"The prostitute is…an outlaw, who controls
the sexual channels between nature and culture."*

~ Professor Camille Paglia.

Preface

How the hell did I get here? One of those drunk and drugged desperate women hanging off men and on to car windows on city streets! Now I'm on the inside, selling myself like a commodity. The rawness of the streets and sleazy clubs, ecstasy, cum, cheap lingerie, groping men has become my bread and butter, rent, food, gas in the car.

This is my story of the humanity of that journey and my sojourn within; of the girls; lifelong friends; the men, boys and gangsters; the drugs: ecstasy, cocaine, meth; the pimps; the super yachts and wealthy businessmen; expensive hotel rooms; private homes; swinger's clubs; high-end restaurants; expensive booze; the fun and good times; the bad times and tragic times; the tears and heartbreak.

Contents

1. Hooking Up
2. The Club
3. Services in the Sex Industry
4. 'Flaps in' or 'Flaps Out'?
5. My First Client: The Giggler
6. Swinger's Clubs
7. Sex, Drugs, Thugs and Hugs
8. Vodka and Caviar
9. Gays, Lesbians and Trans
10. Sports, Scoring and Love Boats
11. Mixing Work and Pleasure
12. Worst Sex, Best Sex
13. The Daily Grind(ing)
14. Getting Out
15. Epilogue

"Let's hook up and just
bring fiery death."

~ Charlie Sheen.

"There are more imperfect diamonds
than flawless stones.
So, what the hell? I'll give it a try…"

~ Ellen Hopkins, Traffick.

1. Hooking Up

I couldn't stand his controlling B-S.

When he hurt me bad I hit back by having affairs on him, to get revenge, and the love and nurture that he couldn't provide. It was the only way I could own anything of myself, retake some sort of control and reassert my personhood. Jason was a jerk. Unreliable and a complete narcissist.

Narcissists are all-consuming, so frustrating, so damaging. They wear you down, eat your soul. You have to hit back, and use extremes to regain yourself.

Being money-driven and loving sex, those two strands began to converge and weave together, and Jason fueled my desperation. I'd driven past The Club for years, thinking, "*I could do that and get paid!*"

I was working in retail nearby and was constructively dismissed. The boss had sexually harassed a younger employee and then hired a girl to replace me. So I took his ass to court and won a payout. But I was still out of a job. I was out of work and out of love, and seriously in debt, with no support from Jason-the-Jerk. Suddenly, The Club seemed really appealing.

Michelle who'd been sexually harassed by the same boss who dismissed me, left with me at the same time. She also got a payout but couldn't get work either. She was younger, 30, I was 45. She wanted to to go to Europe and needed savings.

> "*Why don't we just go and work in a brothel?*"

"Why not!" I said.

The idea gelled. But we were apprehensive. My Christian upbringing was shouting from the side lines. I'd always loved *Jesus Christ Superstar* and knew Mary Magdalene, one of Jesus' closest disciples, had been a prostitute. That assuaged any guilt-pins pricking me from my past. So, Michelle and I teamed up together to go through with her silly 'dare.'

We rang. They said come in. We didn't. We left it a few days to pluck up the courage, but I kept driving past the place. It looked nice, ordered, well-designed, tasteful colors. I thought, *"Can't be all that bad."* It had been there for years, so was obviously a reasonably well-run place, part of the community. I didn't want flashy risky stuff, rather, something solid and reliable. The Club on Solvent Street seemed to settle in my mind as a benefactor who could help me out. A 'Sugar Daddy.'

I was seriously in debt with bills mounting and no chance of getting a settlement with Jerk after 12 years (and on-and-off for eighteen). Crazy I know, women should get what they are legally entitled to. But sometimes it's not worth the risk. Many women get harmed or killed. That was the price I paid for being free of Jerk.

My kids had moved abroad so I was reasonably free and unattached, despite living with Jerk who was really, as it turned out, only a stop-gap. We lived together, but in separate rooms, no sex, it kind of worked. Except for the narcissistic roller coaster and NPD tantrums. Somehow I'd stayed with him twelve years. My how the years fly and the grind just keeps on grinding. It was time for change.

When Michelle and I rang The Club, a week after our discussion, a woman answered. She was super friendly and welcoming. Her voice was very normal, so housewifey. I'm not sure what I expected, perhaps a cigarette ravaged raspy voice. Her tone was reassuring. We were drawn in. A good start. So we arranged to go in and meet Amanda The Club manager the following Wednesday (hiring day).

Hanging up the cellphone, Michelle and I looked at one another, cross-legged in her flat, excited, nervous. *"What the hell are we doing?"* It had been a half serious dare. But somehow, we were now resolved, repelled and attracted all at the same time. I'd never done anything like this. Sure, I'd had lots of guys after high school and had been married since 21 that had lasted a decade. And then another long term relationship. Things were different now. Horizons were opening; new vistas beckoned and I really needed some money. Fast.

The following Wednesday, Michelle and I met in the carpark of The Club and walked in together, through a discrete back entrance. Ushered into a back room with another girl, the three of us sat there like expectant debutants for our impending interview.

The room was dark, old school, themed vintage furniture, mirrors, dark stained wood, tasteful. There were posed erotic pictures on the walls, but nothing seedy or over-the-top. This was erotic not orgy, themed not 'back alley.'

Our fellow traveller was an exotic girl, maybe 20, plain, a bit over weight for her age. We chatted but mainly Michelle and I were talking about our work names. As soon as we'd been ushered in, Amanda the manager had told us to come up with a working name, like celebrity musicians or actors.

I chose *Jasmin*, Michelle chose *Millie*, but later she had so many creepy guys, she had a cluster of working names to avoid being stalked. We sat there for maybe half an hour, eventually Amanda came back and took us in to a main office. We passed near a bar where lots of guys were drinking on bar stools. They leered at us. Fresh fish in the pool. They were men who came in on interview days (Wednesdays and Thursdays) to view the new girls in the hope of "getting her first."

We sat in soft chairs in the office. Opposite us were two people behind a desk: the owner, an older man and a middle-aged woman who did all the marketing and advertising. Just normal people in a normal office.

Peter the owner, started the interview. He had a nice demeanor. I found out later, one of the few owners who didn't insist on screwing the new girls to see what they were like. I had nice legs, great boobs, a tan, and was wearing a close-fitting mid-thigh dress. Peter asked me to stand up and lift my dress higher. I tentatively did, an inch. "*Higher*" he said. Another inch. My dress showed off my figure and and I'd come with a low cut because obviously I wanted to look sexy. Peter just said, "*You look great, you'll do"* and I dropped the dress back down, like that scene in *Bombshell* when Peter Ailes asks anchor-to-be Kayla Pospisil to lift her skirt up to her crotch inch by inch.

I was shy, yet in a brothel auditioning to be a prostitute. Stupid I know, but I've always been a bit shy about my body and didn't know these people. I knew I was going to have to sleep with all sorts of men - and as I learned, women and Trans, even Dwarves, as well - but I was still nervous about lifting my dress up to my crotch for Peter. I didn't know this owner, and felt on display, which of course I was. I was now a commodity and they were checking out their stock. I learned later that as I left, the woman had said,

> *"She's too old, she's no good."* But Peter had replied,

> *"No, she's sexy she'll do great."*

He was right.

I was actually surprised he didn't ask me to strip. I liked that, as I'd heard most owners like to try the girls out before they start. Free sex, a kind of control-dominance thing I suppose. It made me feel this guy was worth working for and the establishment was not going to exploit me. They did ask, "*Do you want to start straight away, go on the floor and start working, do your thing?*" We both said no, and started two days later. Neither of us were mentally ready. We'd both gone for an interview and were not expecting to have to start. I wasn't going on the floor in what I was wearing, for a start. That shows how naive I was. We just had no idea we could start like that. But of course, they just want girls on the floor, especially new girls, because there are guys there waiting, salivating for the new chicks. Predators.

The Club makes 50% on every booking, so it's good quick money. Of course we are being exploited. But we're consensual; we're willingly selling ourselves, our bodies, to men (and women) through the establishment. It's a mutual circle of money-making.

They explained some of the 'dos and don'ts,' like not seeing clients after hours under any circumstances, how to look after our health, check-ups, and took us on a tour of The Club.

"Every time a man knocks on
a brothel door,
he is really knocking for God."

~ Gilbert K. Chesterton.

2. The Club

Throughout The Club there was an old carpet like you see in those old hotels, that last for decades. The walls were lightly colored, a pastel tone, with sexual images on the walls where the action took place. Tastefully done. Contemporary and classic images. But in the areas where sex takes place there are more mirrors.

Very low lighting, lights on dimmers. Narrow passageways, actually quite homely rather than claustrophobic. It felt interesting; the colors, the textures, the pictures. I liked it. I felt comfortable there, more than I did in minimalist modern hotels or fancy apartments owned by rich guys with no taste.

There's a bar in the middle of a large room surrounded by maybe a dozen bar stools. Behind a cut-out partition is the lounge area, next to the bar through which the clients sitting at the bar can view the girls and vice versa. This is where they pick out the girls or come in to the lounge area and select a girl.

The lounge has a couple of long couches and tables with bar stools not designed for comfort rather to encourage the guys to book quickly not hang around., There might be 15-20 girls in there lounging, but mostly milling about introducing themselves to clients, chatting. Most of the vibe was like a stand-up cocktail party. The couch was supposed to be left free for clients to relax, view and chat with the girls. This is the pickup area which is free. The object is the girl is trying to get booked for an hour. A client could sit there for an hour and just chat to a girl for free. If they were good drinkers they could probably do that, but if they weren't, no bookings, the managers would tell them to book a girl or leave. This was a place of business and transaction, despite the ambient pleasantries.

When clients arrive, if they're new, they are met by a manager who pulls them aside into the room we first came in to. If they've been before and know the drill, they just go straight to the bar or lounge and get a drink.

There are two 12-hour shifts, and each has two managers; one working the floor, the other taking the money. Two women. It was always women, not men, when I was working. Clients seem to like working with women, and the women know the girls better than a man.

    "I want a dominatrix!"

    "Oh, Holly would be great with you."

Or

    "I want a girlfriend experience!"

> "Let's pair you up with Jasmin, she's great; you guys will be perfect together."

Managers also get feedback from clients,

> "Jasmin was great, she was perfect for that,"

Or

> "Cheryl was useless at kissing, and her blow job was just awful, I won't book her again."

The manager's job is quite involved and important. She needs to know the girls and the clients; what services they provide; and if they do a good job. It's not her job to pair clients and girls up, but to suggest a business coupling. Sometimes a client might just want a look: a black girl; a plump girl (popular, actually). Managers get to know their floor, their girls, the regular clients, and help 'grease the pole' if you'll excuse the shop pun.

A new client gets a run down in that side room on how things work. A flat rate per hour for normal full service which is quantified and explained (full penetration intercourse, kissing, fondling, massaging, hand-job, blow-job, etc). That's your standard service.

Extras are always, well, extra. More for anal sex, breast feeding, role playing or dominatrix for an hour. Although the price can vary if the girl is doing a good job, she might demand extra.

There's not a lot of negotiation or discussion. Mostly, guys just come in, look around the lounge, pick a girl they like. Both of them go to the booking office, which is close to the bar. The manager will hand him a sales terminal. If a guy is booking a girl for several hours, he wants to pay in cash, rather than by sales terminal, because it's cheaper. And girls preferred cash although cash was always being stolen.

Once that's sorted, we go to a room, but he might say,

"I wouldn't mind trying anal."

"Well that's extra, darling, if you want anal."

Generally the girls negotiate or moderate price. For example, some, like me, don't like anal. We would only do it for a lot more money. Others want extra for kissing. I allowed kissing as part of the standard charge, so I'd get more bookings, but other girls were particular.

There are toilets upstairs for the girls and downstairs for the clients, but everyone generally used whatever.

There's a kitchen area where girls can chill and receive food orders, a down time area away from clients and the pressure of getting booked, where they can smoke away from every one. Generally the smoking took place in the rooms during a session after intercourse.

The rooms is where almost all of the action takes place. There is a corridor in between, which might be used for public humiliation play, say leading a guy down there on all fours, leashed and collared. I did that several times. Off the corridor are several rooms, a bit smaller than an average bedroom. A queen size bed dominates against a wall and every room has a large shower cubicle in one corner with a basin. Some rooms are bigger than others. Larger rooms would be booked if there was a three or foursome. There are rooms upstairs and downstairs.

There was a discrete entranceway, a side room, an office area, a bar and lounge, a hallway, upstairs and downstairs sex rooms, a chill out area for girls and a smokers' area, and toilets.

The beds in the rooms were covered in a mock-vinyl so they could be easily cleaned. But this meant The Club sometimes smelled of a mix of disinfectant, cigarette smoke, spilt alcohol, dope. You got used to it as did the clients. Some girls lit scented candles or incense to remove odors or to make it more erotic or romantic and played their own music to feel more at home.

We were told the nitty gritty, like the hours of a shift (usually 8-12 hours, and a day or a night shift. I selected the latter, because you earn more). 10am - 6pm or 6pm - 6am. Bookings obviously could go over a shift time, but generally the cleaners came in at 6am, and that's when girls clocked off.

Some girls did shorter shifts, working around children, so schedules were flexible. It was all about the bookings, but there was a roster. You weren't on a clock, you and the club earned a negotiated fee for a booking. So, you could be sitting around all night earning nothing.

That happened a lot. It pissed us off, but usually I'd get booked. It could be one client for ten hours ($3000) or five clients for an hour each. You always try to get extensions, that is, longer bookings. Ten clients for an hour each would do my head in because you have to shower between every client. So you're constantly showering, like twenty showers a night, if I had ten clients. On average I'd have six clients a night shift, so 12 showers.

You always shower with the client at the beginning of a booking, using the room shower. This is how things begin. It's a hygiene thing and a good standard way to start things off. The girls would usually wash the client, to make sure they wash properly. Often clients would not want to shower, because it's using up their hour (despite the fact they're showering naked with a beautiful, usually younger, woman. Hell-o!?). Clients often reeked of B.O. and we had to be careful of 'crabs,' other STDs, and open wounds (i.e. AIDS or hepatitis). Self protection.

We learned about "extensions." That's when a client books a girl for a negotiated session on a set-price. The industry is all about up-selling and creating added value which can be charged for.

The Club had an intercom to every room. This was the 'buzzer' and was used if I needed the accessory box sent up for extras or a sales terminal for the client to pay for extras.

There is music playing throughout the club. Grinding bad language sexual music: *Rihanna*, *Eminem*, *Black Sabbath*. It was varied, raunchy, energetic, sometimes soft and quiet, anything to do with sex or love. You'd also use the buzzer to get the office to maybe turn the music down (which is piped to every room) or maybe your client wanted it turned off altogether.

There is also an emergency button if we needed it (and could get to it) and were unable to use the buzzer (like if the client was standing in front of it, or something). This sends a room alarm to Security, who come immediately. The boys will open the door (they have keys) which are snubbed usually so you don't get interrupted. They come, sort out whatever is going on, protect the girl.

I've never had to use the alarm, but others have.

We learned what escorts do. Girls don't just have sex in their club. We get invited out to restaurants, on to super yachts, back to guy's places, to swinger's clubs. It's varied. The Club keeps 'clicking the ticket.' Girls do 'privates' on the side, but that is discouraged. It happens and The Club turns a bit of a blind eye, but they did tell us it was dangerous. It can be. That's where girls get killed, on the streets, in cars and shady public sex spots.

> "Don't do privates, because with us you have security."

Some did privates but not all. I did privates a couple of times a month, because the money is much better. Remember, I'm doing 12-hour shifts five times a week. The clubs get suspicious if you're not on shift, out doing privates all the time. So, I kept it discrete and rare and chose good-paying clients. I had one or two on the side. I'd drop my night shifts back. This gave me more time to do privates with my club regulars, but generally I was just too exhausted and used that time for myself to recover. Paid Love is exhausting, both physically, mentally, and spiritually. I get this, especially as now I'm a Christian. Entering another person is a deeply spiritual thing. As the Bible says, *"The two shall become one."* That's what happens at the moment of intercourse. It's the most intimate physical moment between a man and a woman, and they exchange their femininity and masculinity with one another ("become one"). Not the physicality of sex, but the spirituality. We're alway seeing this. That's why pornography is such a crock and ruins people. They're looking for that connectedness, that soulfulness, spiritual wholeness. People think they can get it through being physical, predatory, fucking as many men or women as they can. But it leaves them empty and frustrated, because they're missing the soulfulness of it all.

My body got exhausted doing night shifts, like truckers, security workers and utility workers well know. It's hard. But escorting is also hard physically. Some guys are rough, there's lust, passion. They might be banging away on me for an hour, so I always made excuses to have a cigarette, go to the loo, just to get a break. I'd get him to order in some drinks or some food.

We were taught about the bar patrons' behavior, what to accept, what not to. A lot of them don't book. But they'd buy us drinks or massage our shoulders. If The Club was quiet we might sit there and talk to them. Generally we were told to stay away, because they're deadwood taking up bar space for paying clients. They could also be critical and discuss girls within earshot which undermines the vibe and disturbs the girls. Owners don't like it. It's corrosive. That was explained to us. But you get thick skinned in the game. On the flip side, mostly you're praised. My ego was boosted through the roof not to mention my confidence and self esteem.

I actually felt good a lot of the time because my confidence was really lifted. I certainly got more praise, adulation, devotion and sexual attention at The Club than I ever did at home. For many women that is addictive. It's also why many of them join the industry. And why many older women are serial online daters. I call those gals 'Hover Flys;' constantly moving from flower to flower addicted to their feelings of being attractive and a man chasing them. "The chase." But as soon as they have sex (conquer there guy) they lose interest and are back online, hooking up the next paid restaurant dinner. After all, it's why girls stay with narcissistic husbands or guys who beat them. It's a bit like playing childhood "catch and kiss" at grade school. Once you catch them, what do you do? Start chasing and screaming again. It's all about the chase and being alluring. The journey not the destination.

Before Michelle and I left on that first day, the services The Club offered were explained to us in detail, that is, the stuff we could be booked for or would have to do.

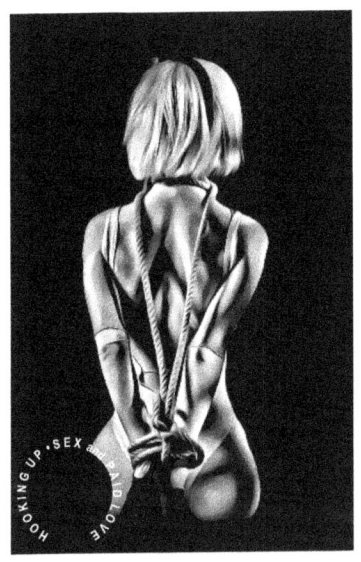

"I believe that sex is one of the most beautiful, natural, wholesome things that money can buy."

~ Steve Martin.

3. Services in the Sex Industry

Girls can specialize, depending on what they are into, what they like, or don't like, or are prepared to do (for money, it's always about the money). Some offer ordinary sex, or something more intimate and caring.

Kissing

Kissing is negotiated because in many ways it's more intimate than intercourse, as I mentioned. You can zone out during intercourse (the old adage "*Lay back and think of England*") but not when kissing. Your eyes are facing one another. There were actually times when we were on our phones while the client was banging us. You just hold it up behind his head or if he's doing you doggy-style, down in front of you. But don't get caught.

With kissing, you can't do that. You can also get gum disease, as I did. Condoms tend to protect you with intercourse, well 95% of the time. There's no protection with kissing. If I gave a blow job, the client had to wear a condom. The thin rubber often irritated my mouth. I was doing a bi-girl once, and she was told to go down on me. She put a condom over her tongue and tried to lick me out. The client was not impressed.

Clubs generally offer clients "whatever turns them on" and let's face it, men fantasize about all sorts of things. Services were advertised, but basically you could call up and anything was on offer, if a client and escort could negotiate a price. Your wildest fantasies could come true (for the right price). That was the exchange. The manager would then pair up a girl with a client. *"Jasmin does really good girl friend experience"* so she'd be paired with Client X. But clients usually picked the girls, like younger looking girls for a "schoolgirl" service. That's usually how it went.

French Kissing

French kissing is passionate tongue kissing. This is an extra, because kissing is very intimate and exposing, and often a booking may not include kissing if a girl declines it, as many did.

Anal

There was 'back door' (receiving or giving anal sex). This could be with a strap-on or a dildo. You do the guy up the ass or he does you, or with his own cock as long as he wears a condom. Anal is an extra charge whether you're giving him anal or he wants to give you anal (which is a choice the girl has). I generally didn't allow anal for the rate The Club was charging but did give it for a much higher negotiated fee on very rare occasions.

I knew a gay proctologist and he hated the weekends. because gay guys would come in with all sorts of anal problems, damage. Chair legs, broom handles, bottle brushes, tubes with hamsters in them. Often times things broke or got stuck and he had to repair his patients. The anus has quite sensitive soft tissue which is why it's so popular with gay and lesbian partners and some heterosexuals. But it's always messy even if you fast from food before hand.

The Club was trying to charge a lot less for this service at the time. I disputed it. Giving anal is really unpleasant, even if using a strap-on. There can be shit on it, so you condom the strap-on as well, that way it's easier and cleaner and you don't have to wash the strap-on afterward. Just invert the condom like a doggy poo bag, and toss it in the bin. Management thought it was no big deal, because they're not the girls doing the job. They didn't understand.

They also tried to drop the price (the girls' price, not The Club's) on long bookings. I disputed that too, because the girls are still doing the same work. I got hauled in to the office the next day about that, so had to sit down and explain to management my point of view.

Their argument was we got taken to spas, and out for dinner and that was a form of 'payment.' But that is all on our time and shouldn't be considered 'payment.'

I wouldn't be going out for dinner or having spas with these guys if I was on my own time. It's also the clients making the suggestions where we go, so that's on them. I was there to earn money. It's different if you and the client negotiate a cut rate, but it's not the club's right to *carte blanche* discount girls without their consent from taking their full cut, when it's the girls giving their bodies to men to use.

You don't give your body in exchange for food or drink. That's slavery.

Fisting

I fisted guys and was fisted in return (but only in my vagina). I never wanted to be fisted anally. It was not necessarily a gay thing, although obviously it's a big part of gay sex. Heterosexual men loved being fisted or fisting. I loved being fisted vaginally. It creates a really intense long orgasm. It's a natural extension of being fingered, which creates arousal and orgasms (especially if guys know where a woman's g-spot is) and it can progress to fisting, which simply extends the arousal and orgasm and can maintain it.

Penal penetration stops after a man comes (he "comes down") and most often he becomes flaccid (unless using viagra). So fisting can maintain arousal for a woman, because her partner is effectively hard all the time and can stay hard. It's very intense. A fist is three times the size of a cock, so maybe I would have 15-20 minutes of intense sexual pleasure, arousal, but it gets too intense and I needed to stop. The orgasm gets too much. Normally I'd have an orgasm and the feelings would dissipate, "I'd come." But with fisting, it's ongoing, it's too intense, and I just had to stop.

A young guy was fisting me. We'd been going about 15-20 minutes. (I'd continually squirt lube into position, while the sexual activity is going on). He began by fingering me internally and it just developed into fisting. It's not like a punch fist, more like a hand mimicking a birds head, so the hand slips in easily, and is pushed further in. With fisting you can go further than a penis can (depending on how long a penis is).

I was on my back initially but as it got more intense I rolled over on his fist. I was trying to change positions so it wasn't so intense.

Eventually I just had to crawl off the bed and pull myself off his fist to stop the intense sex. We didn't actually have intercourse, just fingering and fisting.

Prostitution is mainly intercourse, missionary or doggy-style, cowboy or reverse cowboy [1] about 70% of sexual activity; 30% is other (talking, anal, fisting, wanking, bondage, etc).

Fisting, can be either vaginal or anal. It's up to a girl but obviously a guy would be anally fisted (I never saw a girl being anally fisted, because it's extremely damaging) and the client would fist a girl vaginally.

There's a heavy cost to this as girls who did too much anal sex (not fisting) become stretched and in some

---

[1] "Cowboy" is the woman riding the man's cock on top, facing him; he is the horse. Reverse cowboy is where she faces his legs and pumps him from above, like galloping.

cases have to wear diapers for the rest of their lives. The anus doesn't pull back like the vagina can. You can be vaginally fisted for a time and your body will pull back. But fisting is damaging as obviously neither the anus nor the vagina are designed for human fists.

I quite enjoyed vaginal fisting, it was extremely arousing because it was really intense. The friction creates sexual intensity. It was a feel good thing, but it got so intense I wanted it to stop. I'd multi-orgasm but it just kept going. Too intense.

The vagina is actually quite large so if you're having a lot of sex, and some men are really large (some races are definitely larger than others) you do expand. A girl might be being masturbated and it can just develop into fisting; part of a standard service, because obviously you might be in the middle of a regular service and fisting develops. It's hard to stop and charge an extra levy. It's also the girl's prerogative and if she allows it, then that's on her.

In my case, I told the manager "*yes*" and she said, "*fantastic service,*" and then I got more clients because it's a male fantasy, and there is the possibility by booking me they could get fisting. She tended to then book me as a girl who liked being fisted. I got a bit of extra work, but I stopped offering it because it was too intense and I was worried about vaginal damage.

Clara did a lot of vaginal fisting. We girls were in the smokers' room one night between bookings and were talking about fisting and vaginal size. Clara said,

> "*I could probably put my phone up my vagina.*"

> "*Do it!*" I said, being me.

So she did, being her. But then I rang it...and we all cracked up.

> "Clara! There's a call on your line. It's Clitoris! he's pushing your buttons."

> "Get him to 'ring' you!"

> "Is it a collect call?"

It went on like that all night.

This is what we did between bookings. We'd laugh a lot, play practical jokes, exchange dark sex humor, look after one another. A girl would be getting screwed by two guys one minute with a third cock down her throat, and the next minute she's out back with us playing *Candy Crush* on her phone. They were really just girls, but of age to have sex. Physically able but mentally and socially quite immature. I felt quite motherly towards many of them, except they were my competition for bookings, unless we were a bi-girl team.

Girls caught up quick. In this game, you grow up real fast, because you're dealing with humans intensely, up close and often, perhaps more than any other industry.

I came to really admire a lot of the girls. They were legends. Mothers with children just trying to make ends meet, to get ahead; or girls with really useless partners who lived off their wives or partners, whom the girls (like me) were too afraid to leave because violence was real. A girl could get really smashed up, hurt, or even killed. You read about it in the papers all the time. If you'e mixing drugs, sex and alcohol, with gangs and other vice, corruption, well it's all hand-in-glove. That's why I would never work the streets.

A *Government Benefit*'s agent told me at the beginning,

"Just go work the streets, it's quite safe."

She was married to a cop, and they'd drive up and down the streets. She had no idea. Next week one of the girls was found in a river.

Threesomes

In terms of having two men at once, a threesome (two men and one woman), I mainly did those because I was one of the few brave enough to have two cocks at once. And I did, literally. Sometimes I'd have two cocks in my vagina. One client would be on his back and I'd be laying on him horizontally and the other client would be doggy-style on top of me from behind. I'm sandwiched in between, two guys fucking me simultaneously. It's not intimidating because of the humor factor. It can be difficult physically, cocks are different sizes or because they're drunk and they're not as hard as they think they are.

Being double-fucked is tight. It's not as intense as the fisting, even though two cocks are probably about the same size, and a fist can sometimes go further, but it's the pleasure of two men giving dedicated attention to my body. It was more of a drunk fun thing to do, a dare. The clients would be friends, good mates, egging one another on to do one girl, in the bar. They'd both have to pay for me, so it's a double booking.

Understandably I went for those, maybe four or five times total, as it's unusual and awkward but you get paid twice for one lot of sex. More commonly, I'd be doggy-style, with one guy banging me from behind, another client doing me orally at the front. That was more common because usually a foursome would be two guys in a room with two girls having separate conventional sex.

Double-fucking is awkward though, two men thrusting at the same time, so it turns in to a laugh and kind of falls apart and everyone laughs.

"*That was awesome, Jasmin!*"

"Yeah Jasmin."

"*Yeah fellas you were great, jump in the shower.*"

We might have a chat, a cigarette and then just go, and I do the usual room cleanup for the next girl.

On one occasion, me and Bella were having a threesome with a guy. The client fell asleep, which was common after lots of sex and alcohol. Having a naughty fun nature, I took a chocolate bar from the vending machine, and pushed it up his anus, where it melted. We thought this was hilarious. When he woke up, he thought he'd shat himself and was really embarrassed. He showered and left, probably wondering what had just happened.

Pulling practical jokes was a way of lightening a night, especially if you had hardcore clients, guys who'd bang you for an hour (which is hard work) who were too serious and worked you really hard.

I had a big strong client who used to come in early in the morning, about 4am, after he'd been to an all-night gym. He was quite intense and would set his stop watch on his phone the minute we were in the room and refuse to take a shower. He wanted to fuck me hard for the whole hour. He'd do me hard, then flip me over roughly and take me from behind, and then flip me back again and do me hard on my front, then hard on the floor, then up against the wall, with no break. It felt like he' been through a sex book and wanted to use me in all the positions he'd studied. He was relentless, hyped up from the gym, probably on steroids, and never stopped. I felt bruised and black and blue. It was exhausting.

He had me once a week for several months, and it was too much at that time in the morning, after I'd been working since 6pm the night before. On the last occasion with him, I walked out. I couldn't put up with that attitude any more and passed the booking on to another girl. I never saw him again after that.

Spanking

Spanking (receiving or giving or both). This was usually hands or a paddle. Normally the client does the spanking but sometimes he might enjoy being spanked.

I tolerated spanking. A client might book me but they never asked for spanking beforehand because that might put a girl off. Clients would get in the room and then say they wanted to spank you, *"Not hard, just gently."* But it always was.

I'd usually agree, depending on the client (if I knew them as a repeat; or their look; or just my gut instinct) because I wanted to keep the booking. It was also an extra.

The manager would hand me the case, I'd open it up, the client would select what he wanted to use. Usually there were two or three whips or paddles to choose from. Sometimes the client would use his hand. That can hurt. We'd never allow a belt, because it's damaging. It's a dodgy area, because male sexual drive can get up, get excited, and what starts as gentle can easily –and usually does– escalate. You can go with it, especially if you like the client, or he's attractive, or paying really well, and you can get stirred up yourself. Adrenalin kicks in and away you go. But you have to be careful.

I'd position doggy-style on the bed or bend over the bed, as instructed. Or over his knees. And the client just spanks you. It goes on until you plead with him to stop, and usually they do, sometimes not, in which case you crawl off them.

One time my ass was red, nearly bleeding. I crawled off and he ordered me back on to the bed, doggy-style. I told him, "No, I'll call Security!" and he relented. They're already a little bit ashamed or guilty, spanking, unless they're hardcore, so it's easy enough to get them to stop.

It can really hurt and you just go until you can't take it any more or don't want to. You terminate that activity and just have sex, or distract your client, inviting them to do something else.

You can't allow severe discipline, because it affects your ability to take another booking. You're too sore, bruised, you need time out which is all down time and no pay.

Your bum can be so sore you can't even sit down and that affects your professional ability for a follow-on booking, which is what all girls are focussed on. Paid Love is a callous conveyor belt. Sales, client in, client out (literally and figuratively).

I hated spanking, it was never gentle despite promises. It made me feel degraded, humiliated, and annoyed I'd agreed to it, to keep a booking. So, I'd avoid it, but sometimes it just happened. Eventually however, I just stopped taking those bookings.

> *"Nah, let me give you a really sensual massage. Come on Baby, let me lead; I'll make it worth your while."*

Girls actually have a lot of power. Most men melt when a woman comes on like that and will allow them to work their feminine charms.

Bondage

I didn't mind doing light bondage as a threesome, with another girl, where we tie the client's hands behind his head, tie his ankles together, gag him, blindfold him using soft materials. We'd then both play with him; put nipple clamps on him and he might ask us to whip or smack his cock with our hands.

We'd talk it up a bit, kind of bossy, a bit dominatrix. If he was squirming or talking too much, we might bark at him to shut up. It was part of the game that they take it silently, which was easier for us. Much of dominatrix play is verbal and almost all of it for the clients is in their head. Obviously some go full tilt (all the dress ups and gear, furniture and rooms) but that's not the brothel scene in my experience, that's fetish or swinger's clubs with specialist interests and facilities. Regular working girls like me were not usually enamored of that scene. I didn't do it regularly, usually only if I was with another girl booked as a threesome in which case I'd play along.

Dominatrix

If it was going to take place or a client specifically wanted dominatrix-play, they'd book you beforehand for this service. It's like a normal experience except I'd wear a mask I could see through, a lacy mask; put my hair up (normally as *Jasmin* I'd have my hair down as a worker). They'd be laying on the bed, but I'd always have my heels on. I'd have a longer whip, not necessarily whip them, you crack the whip, hit the bed, and be verbally bossy and more abusive than usual. "Sound and fury."

Sometimes I'd take them out of the room, walk them down the corridor cracking the whip; maybe on all fours with a collar and leash. It was really just telling them what to do. The clients seem to like being submissive and being told what to do by an attractive woman. I think this has to do with men who are busy most of their time making decisions, having responsibility, sometimes overwhelmed by demands. Most of our dominatrix clients were businessmen. They can come in to a brothel and there is a sense of relief and relaxation at being controlled, submitting, being told what to do and simply complying. They can relax in to it; everything is decided for them and they just play.

Pain also creates endorphins which is what heavy bondage people are seeking. In Russia and other colder climates, people sometimes plunge in to ice holes and haul out into a steam tent where they thrash one another with switches to draw the blood back to the surface. This creates an endorphin response, akin to an orgasm. And we all know the sexual innuendo and hinted pleasure of school house beatings and thrashings, especially by "matron."

It can be a bit much to call this deviant. Of course, some of the excessive stuff is (watch any porn channel and you'll see disgusting, degrading things). But generally bondage and discipline, as opposed to sadomasochism, is play acting, stepping out of your reality, getting stress relief, and having a good time with an endorphin affect thrown in that some confuse with an orgasm.

Obviously many clients come under this service; but mostly they don't. It's mostly a brain fuck.

I feel it's a *ying* and *yang* thing. Everyone needs balance in life, and for some men or professional women, they have many demands and sometimes need a space where roles are reversed, and they don't have the pressure of all the decision-making. A recent Kinsey Institute study found that as well as being centered around sensuality, dirty talk, and risk-taking (such as public sex), common human sexual fantasies center around changing power dynamics.

Being under someone else's complete power can be quite relaxing. Obviously there has to be trust, but giving yourself completely to another, whom you trust, and just going along with whatever, especially if you are pressured, busy, and responsible all the rest of the time, is a beautiful release. (How popular was that book and film series, "*50 Shades of Grey*"?). It's like a holiday. I think that's mainly what bondage and discipline is, at least at the level I experienced it.

I'd have a dress on and heels and take them back to the room and play out a verbal pantomime. Generally they wouldn't come, they weren't there for that. I didn't like this work, it was degrading. I don't like degrading clients or being degraded myself; I specialized in the girlfriend experience which was about giving the guys a good time. I was at the opposite end of the spectrum.

But I get that some people get off on being degraded, so some girls specialize in that. There are special bondage and discipline clubs, fetish clubs for that kind of sexuality.

There was a special club in the city I worked called *Roma*. Most of the clubs like that went under during Covid lockdown, so it all went online and live. I was taken with a client a few times to this specialist club, which was a dungeon with a bar. We didn't do anything, just went for a visit.

You go down steps off the street into a big room, brick walls, bar along one wall, along the other wall there are shackles, whips, canes hanging off the bricks. There were dressing rooms. When clients came out to play, it was opposite the bar, and anyone at the bar could watch. This appeals to voyeurs and exhibitionists.

Sex Lessons

Sex lessons could be offered; how to be intimate with a human body, improve your sex.

Sex therapists would occasionally refer their clients to The Club. They'd talk to the manager to find someone suitable. I being mature, older, and a specialist in "girlfriend' was chosen quite a bit. I'd sit there on the bed, naked, and we'd chat. Often we'd never have sex, but I'd stroke him on his shoulder, down his back; just sensual touch. I'd let the client talk. I'd play with his cock. We'd kiss and I would try and get him to get hard by playing with myself while he watched. Many of these guys have been addicted to porn, so doing that can get them excited and hard. So, you mimic what they are used to, which is a screen with porn on it. But porn makes many guys impotent or unable to perform because reality rarely mimics porn. Like trying to live a

TV drama. Real sex can then become disappointing and less stirring, so they can't get it up anymore.

The therapists were interested in knowing if their clients could get an erection with a real person, rather than screen porn, to help them with their sexual addiction counseling with this client. In that sense, we were providing a valuable clinical service, helping therapists and clients diagnose and determine the level of their dysfunction.

This is why I hate porn so much.

MILF

MILF was popular ("Mothers I Like Fucking," that is older woman, cougars. Younger men really like older women -

'mothers'). [2] I was the oldest at The Club (45) but lied about my age (40). I became popular because of my age, a very desired MILF. I had clients aged 20 to 80+.

Multi-shot Orgasm

Multi shot is when a client is allowed to come several times, ie you have intercourse several separate times through the hour. A manager might say to a client,

> *"You can come as many times as you like!"*

> *"That's awesome!"*

Role Playing

Role playing is fantasy play; usually the client pretending

---

[2] MILF is a generic acronym used by adolescent boys about mates' attractive mothers or older sexually desirable women. It is also a popular porn genre and widely searched.

he's a young boy and the escort a mistress or a mother. And we nurture. Guys on a leash; dress ups: clients would bring clothes in and both would dress as nurses and doctors, cops, etc., whatever their fetish was. They'd dress up or you'd dress up, or both. Schoolgirls, cops, nurses, doctors, pilots, medieval, babies with diapers on.

Some clubs have a dungeon of various descriptions for bondage and discipline play, a particular fetish. Other clubs aren't set up for that, they just do sex. The kinky stuff would take place in the rooms.

Maybe a client is tied and whipped using toys The Club has for that purpose. Gags, blindfolds, ropes, handcuffs, dildos, strap-ons, not chains because our club didn't have anywhere to secure such things. A specialist club is where those clients would go.

Nude Massage

I'd done a massage course so did a lot of this and I'd get repeat service. I'd always end with sex, "finishing off" as we call it. I'd massage naked. Just intercourse. I enjoyed this. It was hard work (I could massage for 30 minutes or more non stop) because it was less involved. Clients liked the physical contact, the intimacy, the sensuality, being nurtured. It has less of the sexuality than banging and is perhaps more intimate between two people.

Bi-girl (Two Girls, One Guy)

Two-girl bi is when a client books two girls and watches them have sex with one another. He's paying for the service, in which the girls have to perform as lesbians for his entertainment. So it's extra. It includes sex with him, but that's a threesome which would be less. He's paying a bi-rate. Often we'd fake it. We'd really kiss, but if we had to go down on one another (oral) we'd put our hand over their pubes or use our hair to cover up. But if the client pulled our hair back and wanted to really watch, then we did what we were paid for, and he'd often join in. So we tended to team up, go with a fellow girl we knew and didn't mind having sex with.

A client might book me and I'd get to choose another girl to go with. But sometimes they'd say *"I want Jasmin and Charlotte,"* and we'd just have to have sex with one another.

It can be awkward, because you don't know your colleague's boundaries; can't read their body language as well, so it's better to team up over time and go through the routine as a team, performing sex or faking it together, understanding one another's routines, like tight rugby combinations. Speaking of which, I had several national sportsmen, well known guys, and other celebrities. But I'll never disclose names. That's cowardly and unfair; they payed, often more for discretion.

If you just get forced into a two-girl bi, a girl might have a thing where she just gives pecks. But the guy might want full on female tongue kissing. If she demurs, clients might tell a girl off. I'd just say, *"Get into it, just do it!"* I'd encourage them just to be actresses. It's always just business, well was to me, strictly, rarely would the two girls get turned on.

I teamed up with a dark girl and we did well, because guys liked putting a white girls with a dark-skinned girls, the cross cultural, white/dark duality seemed to turn them on. It was mainly kissing and oral sex, or we'd use a strap-on and have intercourse. The client would direct, he might say, *"You put on a strap-on."* This was good, as it usually meant an extension, as we'd run out of time. More drinks would be ordered and the manager would know, so the sales terminal would come up and more money would flow.

We'd always break the session up, have a cigarette, drinks, the clients would like to boast about their lives, what they did for jobs, flash houses, cars, travel, and we'd use this to break up the sex. Because girls can't just have sex with one another for hours on end. It would be negotiated in the heat of the excitement, the manager, the girls, the directing client.

"Hey big boy, you're making me really horny, why don't we go for another three hours. I could do this, do that, make a night of it; we could do all sorts of things. How 'bout we go to a swinger's club? Ever been to a swinger's club?"

The client sometimes feels pressured. And if he's drunk, well we can manipulate him time-wise for more money. Other times he's willing and will often initiate an all night 'play.' We often referred to sex as 'playing' and it could include any or all variety of activities (talking all night, intermittent sex, drugs, drinking, massaging, whatever).

It's a popular male fantasy to watch two women having lesbian sex, so it was popular in The Club. But threesomes were more common, as some clients are not in to two-girl bi which is a 'special.'

If he books two girls and all three have sex, that's a threesome. I pushed for bi's because it paid more and was my speciality.

I went home one night with one of my colleagues. We were both very drunk from The Club because we'd both had a night of quite rough sex and several bookings. I took her home with me because I lived in a really nice place and thought it would be nice for her, after our hard shift, just for a change. We drank more and got even more plastered.

My partner came in eventually, from his job. He arrived just as she was going down on me in the lounge (giving me oral sex). In my blurry haze, I looked up and saw him standing there, watching, in his work gear. I felt a bit panicked. I'd been caught doing something I shouldn't. I was worried about being unfaithful to him, outside work (banging at work was different, he got that and accepted it). But having someone at home, outside work was a direct insult to any relationship, let alone a female. I did it because I was drunk, really drunk, but it was just a continuance of what we'd been doing earlier at work, it just flowed over.

We weren't in love, I didn't have the hots for her, we were just comfortable together. The alcohol lubricated our inhibitions. Just physically comfortable familiar humans pleasuring one anther sexually.

We were smashed and went up to the bed, and crashed, and he came in to be with us, crawled in to the middle, and he started playing with her. She didn't want a bar of it, because she didn't like him. She tried to crawl over him, so she was in the middle, so she could cuddle me and turn her back on him. It was the first time I realized she was a lesbian. Sure I'd done plenty of women, but I wasn't a lesbian. But I know this, because later she wanted a relationship with me.

In the meantime, my partner got really insulted and left the bed, stormed out. We just went to sleep.

At breakfast my partner and I talked it through. He was angry at me and confused and didn't know whether to join in or just have a wank while he watched us go at it. I didn't know what to say. I explained I was hideously drunk and it was just a silly one-off. He bought that and nothing was ever said, and nothing more happened. Until I left his ass a few years later sick of his narcissistic bullshit, swinging moods, controlling behavior and threats. I moved out.

Breast Feeding and Breast Relief

Breast feeding is for clients with baby or mummy fetishes. Girls booked for this were often still really breast feeding and had milk which the clients take, and thats a big extra.

Breast relief, is clients fucking between your boobs, and they'd come on your chest, thus (penis) relief on breasts. Foot fetish was similar, in which you'd put your feet together, and they ram their cock between the arches of your feet like two boobs, and come on your feet, breast or body.

BDSM (Bondage and Discipline)

Beginner BDSM is easing a client in to it. A girl who was experienced, perhaps from her private life, would be chosen and paired with a client who had asked to experience this.

Light domination is gentle dominatrix. Always the girl towards the client, his degradation, bossing him. whipping him not the other way around.

School Girl or Asian Teenager Fantasy.

Clients or girls would have costumes, there was actually a rack of clothes in the office. It wasn't something I ever did but I saw girls swanning about as school girls - that's a pretty common male fantasy. Teen girl or Asian teenager, is clients who want girls who look like teenagers. Everyone lied about their age, so 24-year-old girls said they were sixteen.

Foot Fetish

Foot fetish and foot worship is where clients massage, kiss and suck toes or come over your feet or have their cock up between your compressed feet. A lot of girls didn't like this because they weren't in to their feet, didn't feel their feet were attractive. It seems to be a fetish people have or don't.

Girlfriend Experience

Girl friend experience was something I did a lot of, being empathetic as if you were their girlfriend. I was apparently good at that so got paired with guys who wanted a mock girlfriend instead of a prostitute. I liked this because I'd got a lot of repeat business and often we just talked. Familiarity was the key to repeat bookings as long as they didn't get too clingy and friendly, wanting a relationship. Chatting, a massage, getting deep and personal, kissing and sex as a package. The girl couldn't share her stuff with the client, so you'd just make things up. They were after sympathy and the sex would be tender and nice, compassionate. It was easier.

Hand Job

Hand jobs are self explanatory and could be a half hour booking, a service that was also available. Clients often popped in before work, on the way home, lunchtimes, and tended to be businessmen or tradesmen. Just a case of 'getting their rocks off.' Work them off, they're done, they go. It was also for guys who don't want intercourse. Many men consider intercourse cheating on their wives and they won't go that far in a brothel but might need a sexual outlet and are happy to pay for a hand job.

It was not common while out on escort jobs. Handjobs were mainly a club preserve.

Erotic, Golden or Brown Showers (Scat Play)

An erotic shower is just full sex in the shower, with soap or a blow job in the shower. It can often happen as part of a standard booking.

Golden showers is the girl or client urinating on you or you urinating on them. Not so bad in the shower but awful on the bed because urine goes everywhere. If you got booked for a shower, you'd drink a lot of water to be able to piss. Often you'd have a standard booking and he'd ask for a golden shower. Because it was a standard booking, they'd usually have to pay the girl with cash for the extra service on top of a standard service already underway.

For the guys I think it's about degradation of the female which is a male turn on, or it's narcissistic. But I had it done to me and just showered off. I was usually the one pissing on the client. It made them come.

Brown shower (scat play) is when the client wants the girl to crap on him. It's a weird fetish. A client would fly a girl to a certain city, she had to eat a McDonalds at a specific time because it provided the right consistency of shit for the client. He'd come in, she'd squat and crap, and wank him off at the same time. This would cause him to have an orgasm. Then cleanup and go, and she'd be flown home with $2000 in her pocket. Only some girls would tolerate that, only one or two girls. A very particular fetish but not one I was in to.

Pearl Necklace

Pearl necklace, is a guy coming around your neck so his cum looks like beads, like a pearl necklace.

Anal Rimming

Rimming, is licking around the anal passage, either client or girl. It has high risk of transmission, as obviously the anus is an egress of unwanted waste from the body, so licking this area has dangers. An obviously both parties have to be really clean all the time.

Pegging

Pegging, is a girl with a strap-on penetrating her client anally. Or doing a girl at the client's request in a threesome, as long as she is ok with anal, and him watching. Or it could be part of a threesome gig. Pegging can be anal or vaginal, man on man, woman on man, man on woman, it inverts the natural gender roles regardless of genitalia. Essentially it is an adoption of male sexuality applied to any context allowing men to feel what it's like to be done like a woman, and a woman to feel what its like to have sex like a man.

Shaved 'Pussy'

Many men prefer women clean shaved, others 'full bush,' in some cases because clients saw it as pre-pubescent or child-like. This did not necessary equate to booking younger escorts, I got plenty as an older booking, the age transfer was simply in their head regardless of the prostitute. so managers would pair a 'clean shaven pussy' with a client who wanted that fantasy. Incidentally "pussy" was always our term for a vagina, or a "girl," used as a universal generic epithet. I was not clean shaven myself, I had a waxed 'landing strip.' I didn't like clean shaven because of the childlike association. Some girls had shaved 'hearts' or a lightning bolt. My designer 'landing strip' was just a personal preference. Girls decided themselves to shave or not for their own reasons.

Most guys liked a bit of hair down there. The same applied to tattoos. Guys, especially older guys, would ask for a girl without tattoos while others liked it.

It was also sometimes for hygiene. Clean shaven helps prevent 'crabs.' But whatever the reason (fantasy, hygiene, preference) it was always an extra. Clubs were about creating categories of difference, for which they could obviously re-click the ticket. 'Add-ons' was a way of extending bookings, enlarging how much money could be extracted from a client.

For example, I worked threesomes a lot with Bella. We were a good team and often paired up because she, like me, was good at verbally working the clients for more money.

We always got them drunk if possible and worked the extension, for the client to book both of us for two more hours (as long as possible). Some would extend all night, so we'd be on to a big gig each. Good money and the reason we were all there.

If they were drunk clients were most often limp. They were there to come, so they had to get hard. That would encourage an extension. We'd slow the process by drinking, smoking, talking, taking drugs, massaging, suggesting another girl come in (which would get her money but meant the booking might last longer for us, and we'd get sexual breaks while she was active with him).

I was good at chit chat and conversation. I might suggest guys talk about themselves. I'd draw them out and that would often encourage them to extend the booking, because they're enjoying the company. We'd talk boating, work, showing off, and I'd be fore-playing: massaging, kissing, masturbating, encourage a girl on girl or him to watch (more money).

Being Filmed

Some guys like to be filmed while they are masturbating. One of us would do that on our personal phone and we'd play it back to him and add how sexy he looked and how masculine he was, stroke egos. They'd watch themselves and masturbate more, which could extend the booking.

We might film the clients and girls and play that back but we'd definitely delete it immediately. We always had one another's back. It's ok to be filmed in action in the room, watch the video, but always delete, and never send, because then clients would have our phone numbers, a huge 'no no'. We could also be used for online porn. You have to handle that stuff carefully and we always worked with girls we trusted.

If we were on escort, guys might have a laptop open, filming. Security would come in when they dropped us off and check. We were also pretty good at detecting stuff, based on how the client positioned himself or was acting.

If a client had a lot of energy and it was early in the night, we might suggest going to a night club, simply to extend.

"Have you ever done swinging?"

"No,"

"Oh my Gosh you'd love it, let's go…"

and we could extend by several hours on the clock. It's a pretty alluring suggestion and most guys will go for it, if invited to do so by attractive women and they have the money.

Overnighting

Overnighting, is where a client books a girl to stay the whole night with him (8-12 hours generally). This would usually be back to his place or a hotel room or a club room. We'd order food in, smoke, drink all night, some sex, and then sleep together, an ideal booking, because I'm getting payed simply to sleep.

Security would drop us off and come in to the room and check for hidden cameras, open laptops, phones, etc. They'd also pick us up. This was a good point about being on the books of a club, as you had backup and security. I generally would not drink at a client's house as they could spike your drinks and do things you didn't want. Spiking is also dangerous because people can get alcohol poisoning or a mix of substances might react. We had girls going to hospital because they'd been spiked.

Clients paid for my drive time. I was often driven 2.5 hours away, and back, and the client paid. That was such a good gig that I eventually went private on it and drove myself because it would be an all-nighter, and I'd claim the drive time as well. So while I paid for the gas and my time driving, I'd negotiate with the client who I got to know, extras for that and then he paid for a 12 hour overnighter. I did this several times so I had to manage that with my regular club schedule, where I might only get one or two one-hour bookings over a 12-hour shift.

The point about 'privates' is you don't share the fee with the club, while the client pays the same.

A Japanese-American client used to book me. It would be a quality hotel dinner, up to his hotel room for the night, which would include a sleep, and sex on and off, and I'd come away with big cash. I'd really work him for cash. If you want another kiss, it's another $100, or a quick dance naked, another $100, that sort of thing. Money was no object to these guys, so they'd just pay and you'd keep offering varied activity. .

Submission

Submission is dominatrix. You never let the client be dominant, only the girl would dominate the client. Tying, hand cuffs, lots of verbal abuse, commands, telling them off, whipping, caning. It's mainly a verbal game.

Cock and Ball Torture, Penis Pumps

This is sexuality that uses devices such as cock rings, a hard rubber ring you fit on to the cock like a lamb tail ring. Once the penis is engorged, the cock ring prevents the blood flowing back, so it effectively maintains the erection artificially. Another could be added around the base of the balls. This helped get erection, as well. It was basic stimulation, felt good to the client and excited him. It also gave me good access as it pushed the penis and balls out and you can give great oral sex and 'head' like that.

Some guys I just couldn't make hard. I might suggest using a penis pump. It's a plastic tube that goes over the penis, creates suction while you pump the air out. It can help to generate erection, but not always. It was more of a fun thing to do, kind of kinky, maybe pseudo-medical and might excite a client. It was also easier for me than having sex, or having to blow or hand job a flaccid penis for half an hour.

The whole process of explaining all the services to us on that first night, took a couple of hours. As we left, Michelle and I still felt a bit nervous but also excited. We jumped in our respective cars in the carpark and headed off. What a turning point that day was for both of us.

When I first started working I kept a diary because it was all so exciting, different and exotic. But the diary stopped pretty quickly. You get desensitized early on. I had an entry for June 13 *"Oh God, the abnormal has begun to be the normal."* I got used to giving anal sex, swinging, cross dressers, fisting, dominatrix, all the rest of it just became normal.

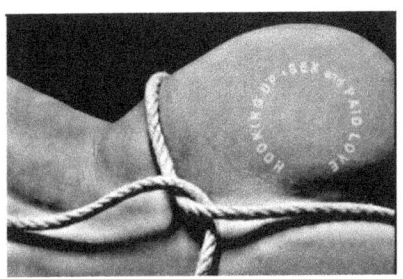

"At her first bleeding, a woman meets her power. During her bleeding years, she practices it. At menopause, she becomes it."

~ Lucy H. Pearce, Moon Time.

4. 'Flaps in' or 'Flaps out'?

Obviously periods are problematic in our industry. But as working girls we had a solution. We would get small round disc-shaped sponges, a very dense sponge and force them up our vagina to block any period emissions. The office had them. They were very effective while a girl was having her period, but they were difficult to remove. They fill up with blood and expand and get jammed in there. Some girls had to go to the doctor to get them removed. But, with one in, you could keep working.

I got one stuck a few times. I knew that oil made them heavy, so I lay down in the shower and squirted olive oil up my fanny. The sponge got heavy, I stood up, and eventually it slipped out.

Having the sponge in made your vagina shorter. If a client had a long cock, he might say

"You're got something up there."

"No, I've just got a short vagina."

Some of the older girls were going through menopause and would get hot flushes. You're supposed to "pause men" with "menopause" but of course they wanted to keep working. Cold showers were good, so I'd tell the client I was really hot, he'd have his shower at the beginning of the booking, then I would have a separate cold shower. That ate up more booking time, but I could also cool off before any action. I'd also have the air-conditioning on cold.

Some clients didn't like that, I just said I'd massage them and warm them up and they really liked that idea. I usually started my bookings with a massage anyway, and clients often came just from my massage. Then of course they weren't concerned with the cold air con.

My parter enjoyed having sex with me when I had my period, because many women actually get more horny. For those of us like that, it was a bonus for the clients. But it also made you very drained, and tired. So although we might be more horny, we were less energetic.

As girls we got adept at reading a client. Were they just in for a quick fuck, in which case, you want it over and done with as quickly as possible inside the hour and collect your fee. So, you might come on to him all horny and enthusiastic, to get him hard and come quickly. Or, you sense he might extend, so you drag it out a bit. Not too much seduction, or allure, but fill it up with chit chat and massage.

We also noticed that we working girls on a shift often got out periods in sync. One would have her period and we would all get ours together, be 'in season' together.

I was putting on my g-string in front of a client after sex, and he said 'flaps in' or' flaps out"? meaning how did I position the g-string. I said *"they tuck in quite nicely"* and we burst out laughing. Even men wear g-strings, so a lot can be tucked away as necessary in the 'overhead locker.'

"Marriage is for woman the commonest mode of livelihood, and the total amount of undesired sex endured by women is probably greater in marriage than in prostitution."

~ Bertrand Russell.

5. My First Client: The Giggler

My first client was a husband struggling with his marriage. He couldn't stop giggling. Perhaps nervousness or anxiety.

As I was to learn in the coming months, the sex industry is often about helping relationships. That may sound disingenuous or oxymoronic, but it's not brothels that break up relationships, it's affairs. Brothels often save marriages. Many clients who come, are in love their wives, but because of menopause, mismatched libidos or stresses at home, there's no sex. It's often been withdrawn, sometimes as a weapon, or it's become boring, jaded or indifferent. Like that scene from the first chapter of Hardy's *The Mayor of Casterbridge:*

"That the man and woman were husband and wife, and the parents of the girl in arms there could be little doubt. No other than such relationship would have accounted for the atmosphere of stale familiarity which the trio carried along with them like a nimbus as they moved down the road." [3]

In the novel, the mayor is taking his wife to market to sell her. We sold ourselves.

Clients (including women) come in to get what they need, perhaps to refresh their marriage. I never really saw it as cheating. Obviously many were, even the girls (on their partners, on The Club, on themselves). But more often than not during the booking, they'd talk constantly about their wife, girlfriend or lover. They wanted to reconnect, they wanted to be in that relationship. They loved them. I spent hours getting

---

[3] Thomas Hardy, *The Mayor of Casterbridge.* Chapter 1.

paid hourly to talk, counsel, sit naked on a bed, no sex, a cigarette, drinks, and talking with a fellow human being about their sorrows, pains, betrayals, frustrations, hopes, dreams and fears.

I was popular for this, as the oldest MILF in The Club I was a natural choice. You couldn't engage meaningfully at that level with a naked twenty-year-old who'd never been married. Managers paired me with those types of clients. It was this that changed my whole outlook on the industry.

Obviously deciding to join a brothel and give your body to strangers is not easy, consequently I remember my first client. After a battle with another girl to get my first job (she was exotic and gave him a lap dance) I apprehensively made my way to the room with him.

He'd had an argument with his wife. He was average height, a caucasian, average build, not unattractive but not Brad Pitt. Dark curly hair, married, like so many of my male clients (and my female clients for that matter, although no penises; but then, there's always pegging). He smelt, so I showered him as all girls did, the default start for any booking. A safety issue as much as anything else. I used my own soap, a tea tree soap because it's highly anti-bacterial, antiseptic and anti-fungal. I'd use that on myself, not waste it on him; he'd get the cheap Club-provided 'hotel' cake.

The showers are in a room corner, and are quite large, much bigger than a normal home shower. A walk in. Brick and tile, stainless steel floor, a single lever tap. There's no glass, just a tile or brick U shape walk-in about six foot deep by 4 foot wide. It's quite a substantial shower unit because it's a necessity (frequently used by two people) and also the starting point for any booking.

I carried a small plastic bag with my tea tree soap in it, grabbed one of his cheap Club cakes from the room side table and suggested to him nicely,

"Why don't we start with a sexy shower?"

His face lit up. I went over and,

"Let's get your clothes off Baby!"

and I started undoing his shirt. Some clients really enjoy being stripped, but usually I'd stop and let them do that, as it's not my thing. While he is stripping, I turned on the shower, let it warm up, and stripped off myself.

I was wearing a matching bra and g-string set with a black singlet dress over the top. I loved these dresses; tight-fitting singlet dresses worked well for me as I was athletic and had a great figure. Also easy to whip on and off. Other girls wore the whole lace up girdle stuff, which takes ages to get off but looks good.

I unbuttoned my bra and took off my g-string, and followed him in to the shower. Later, I'd play up the stripping stuff a bit longer, get the client to undress me and remove my g-string. But generally I was just down to business like on this first booking and stripped off and in to the shower.

We shared the shower, stepped out and dried off and lay on the bed. I asked him what he wanted. He wasn't sure so I suggested we start with a sensual massage, and of course he agreed.

I massaged his back, arms, legs, feet and buttocks while he lay on the bed, then flipped him over and teasingly massaged his chest and finally his cock and testicles gently stroking with fingertips and my tongue. That's when I noticed he had an unusual cock. I hadn't noticed in the shower. It was thick at the base and it came to a point, like a pyramid. I saw one other man like this, years later. A really thick base and a small thick penis terminating in a small head, like a short traffic cone. It was really hard to get the condom on him as it wouldn't go around his base.

Trust me to get this on my first booking.

I persisted and was professional, my first gig after all. After the sensual massage he was happy, smiling and chatting about his wife and their big fight, a bit of a turn off, but hey, I'm a working girl. I straddled him and squatted and gently sat on his cock and fucked him. I worked it verbally,

> "I love your cock Baby, it feels so good, you're so erect, I want to come, fuck me hard!"

He kept giggling, which was a bit-off putting. He came quite quickly. I cleaned him up with tissues, threw them in the bin; he was done, and left.

It's the girl's job to now clean, as part of your booking fee. You spray the vinyl mattress down with disinfectant, wipe it all off with the towels you've used, straighten up, grab new towels from out of the laundry room and set up the room for the next girl's booking: six rolled towels; four soaps; massage oil. Girls bring their own condoms, which you can get free from the health clinics. I'd go through about four or five packs of 12 a month. You just grabbed them when you were going past the clinic or if you had a doctor's appointment.

My male doctor was great. He knew I was in Paid Love and there was never any judgement. He gave me the care and concern I needed and in a game which is so mercurial and callous, you need people like that around you, especially as family can't always be told or are unsympathetic. I had very regular check ups in case a condom split or broke. Incidentally, I caught more STDs off my partners at home, than in the brothel.

You have to manage what you tell family and friends, what you do for a living. For example, what do you tell your kids? Some spouses never knew. Many just said they worked in a night club.

One girl I worked with pretended she was a hotel cleaner and would go off every night to "clean hotels at night." She'd keep her clothes locked at The Club and change in to the working girl, there.

One time a husband wanted to meet his wife, but she'd always deflect by saying, *"I don't know which hotel I'm cleaning tonight and I always move round. I only find out when I get to work."*

Another girl pretended she was just a stripper. Her partner wanted to come in and watch her strip. She told him "no'" in firm terms, that she didn't want him to watch her, it would affect their relationship, and she couldn't strip if he was there.

I wasn't like that. If my partner came in, I had no problem stripping or him watching me have sex. But he never came in.

Another husband who had suspicions, arranged for his mate to go in and check if his wife was a prostitute. She was going through a nasty divorce with him. The mate came in, and asked the girl,

> "Are you Bianca, Peter's wife?"

> "Who?"

She escorted him out the back and as he left he turned and said *"I think you are!"* I was there. I don't know what happened after that. But it must be awful for girls living a lie constantly and having to cover up their daily work from their spouse or partner.

I went back in to the lounge to try and get a second booking. Because it was our first night, Michelle and I were given wine to drink, to help us get through. Michelle already had a second booking so I waited for her and thought about my first night on the game.

It was strange. I wasn't nervous, anxious or afraid. I thought, *"Gee this was easier than I expected, I can do this."* No guilt. I enjoyed it actually. Michelle and I had a good chat, it was easy and such good money. I realized I was going to get my debts paid off in no time. Michelle felt exactly the same, which helped. Having gone in together in the first place, made the decision together as a dare, and completed our first night together (the manager had only rostered us 7pm - 12 midnight, which was usual for new girls) we galvanized and encouraged one another. Lots of girls couldn't do it and they knew that after a single booking or two. Others, like us, coped, even enjoyed it. Some became career girls, even set up brothels themselves, became 'madams' or managers, even advocates. All of them made good money. Some were wise and invested, now own lots of property and investments and are secure in old age. Others frittered it all away on drugs, booze, cars, jewelry, travel and men.

You get a lot of attention in a male dominated environment. It's a real turn on to get all that male attention, compliments, sexual energy, being told you're beautiful, stunning, sexy, all night long, fucked hard, booked over other girls, rebooked, extended and revisited. If you can get past the shame or guilt, it's a great ego boost. And if you add extremely good money on top, for what I stress is normal every day human activity, well, it can be addictive. It's certainly lucrative.

Even now, I miss that aspect, the easy money. There's really nothing like it. When girls leave they have to waitress, wash dishes, clean motels, it's hard long hours for a fraction of what they could wangle from a willing client. As Woody Allen once said,

> "Every hooker I ever speak to tells me that it beats the hell out of waitressing."

And sometimes you get sexually harassed in these low paid jobs; most waitresses have stories, certainly serving bar girls. And if you enjoyed sex, even better.

Most of us were going home to tired relationships, ambivalence, like the *Mayor of Casterbridge's* wife. You don't tend to get the compliments, the adulation which women crave. For any working girls, that's what it's about, the dopamine hit of being adored and fucked by strong males. It's a boost to your femininity. And I don't care what the feminists say, we were far more "empowered" than those Harpies will ever be. And we had enormous power over men, took their money, and manipulated life to our own female ends.

> "The prostitute is not, as feminists claim, the victim of men, but rather their conqueror, an outlaw, who controls the sexual channels between nature and culture." ~Professor Camille Paglia.

For me, as the oldest there, there was definitely a competitive edge. I wanted to be more attractive than the young bimbos, score more bookings, attract more men. And to prove myself to the bosses that I could be good at this.

Two or three months later, I was called into the owner's office for a review, just to see how I was going. The Club can't carry girls who don't get bookings. Peter was full of praise, I think because he'd picked me first over the office women, that I'd be good. He was right.

"Jasmin, you're amazing, you pull the guys. They seem to really like you, you're good money. We're really pleased with how you're going; with how many bookings you're getting."

They'd even do graphs. The managers would ring the owners in the morning and talk about each girl and how many bookings she'd got, how pleasing she was, what she was good at, what the clients were attracted to. A money machine.

I was pleased to have pleased, and being appreciated by the boss. I'd made it. This huge dare Michelle and I took had paid off. I felt a sense of achievement, having done something not many can do. I wasn't promoted in the daily newspaper ads by The Club though, in the personal sections. That hurt a bit, but was actually a compliment in some ways, because I didn't need promoting. I had no trouble attracting men and getting them to book. The ads were designed to bump up some of the lessor achievers and fresh flesh.

But as time went on, I started getting longer escort bookings, and that's where the real money is.

"In the modern world, you could be a swinger, bi, trans, zoo into S&M, but it was forbidden to be old."

~ Michel Houellebecq.

6. Swinger's Clubs

Swinging is more common in particular cities than others. Today, a lot of swinging occurs privately, in provincial towns and outlaying suburbs in well-appointed mansions and properties to which swingers are invited. Some clubs do exist and when I was working, my colleagues and I would regularly use swinging clubs to extend clients. We'd suggest they take us to a swinging club, talk up the salacious details, and off we'd go.

It's also where orgies tend to occur. I attended one with a dozen people or so. Brothels tend to cater for groups of only six to eight people] in one room, "size is everything," as they say. But swingers clubs cater specifically for large numbers of people so orgies can happen.

I went with some clients once. There was a huge low level bed. People oil themselves up or are oiled-up by others (they tend to use olive oil or coconut oil) and then they dive in. There's lots of female cum and oil and it just becomes a writhing mass of bodies. Quite a fun experience actually, surfing slippery wet bodies. Not always a lot of actual sex, it's just about touch and sensuality and the euphoria of being embraced, embracing a huge writhing mass of humanity. The lighting is low. There's a mix of odors, from perfume to room spray, sweat, perfumed candles and the smell of sex.

You feel quite connected. It's like 'riding' at music concerts when a person gets lifted up and passed along by a sea of hands. That's the feeling. It's de-personalized; it's dark; hardly 'people' at all, just human bodies. And men might penetrate you, or you might just suck on cock, or be eaten out yourself by a guy or a woman. No one knows, no one cares.

People would also pair off from the orgy and go to rooms where they'd have individual coupling, threesomes, foursomes, or move in and out of the options. Back and forth.

It was popular as most clients had never tried it. The titillation factor is high, and it was a good advert for The Club. We'd almost always get extension and could sit it out while our client was 'surfing.' Or go to the bar and indulge in an array of cocktails and watch the action from a distance.

Before I began working , I'd known about swinging through some Swedish friends I knew in the tourism trade. They actually pioneered a lot of swinging in this country. They sent an invite out to my husband and I, when they started their first swinging club. We didn't go, but I learned about this sexuality through them. I thought it was weird and wrong.

I don't agree you should go and swing as couples. When you love someone in a committed relationship, my view is you shouldn't share them. That sounds oxymoronic given I started working in the sex trade several years later.

But I never viewed what I was doing (sleeping with others, including other women's husbands, sometimes several at the same time, or with wives) as the same thing. Because it's not about being in a committed relationship. It's just money, a service, and sex. The industry works hard at separating the two.

There are strict rules about not falling in love with clients; not doing privates, and not allowing them to fall in love with you. No phone numbers, addresses and avoiding being followed. Girls are also never allowed to date clients and we're told this strictly from day one.

Their excuse was it was a safety issue, but really, they were losing money because they were no longer a paying client, just a freebee boyfriend on the side. They'd also often lose the girl as well, because the guy knows what goes on - having been a client- and would pressure the girl to stop.

I broke this rule, as did other girls. Mainly because I'm a rebel and independent and can't be told what to do. The relationships almost never work out. A lot of girls lost their jobs because of this, when The Club found out.

It's a game, a charade, we're pantomime. We change our names. Our personas. I was *Jasmin*. At home with my partner, and most girls had partners, we were someone else. I was actually completely different in The Club: strong, angsty, confident, noticed. Outside, I was quiet and often shy, but a nature lover. In nature and the great outdoors is where I am the happiest.

And as I've said, we were often servicing dysfunctional relationships to help save that relationship: a service.

I'll be honest, sometimes having sex with a good looking client, I'd enjoy the sex. Depends on how much I'd been drinking. In this game, drinking relaxes you, it makes you more horny which is why so much alcohol is drunk at clubs, by girls and clients. Booze is associated with sex because it drops people's inhibitions.

> *"Have some madeira, m'dear.*
> *You really have nothing to fear.*
> *I'm not trying to tempt you, that wouldn't be right,*
> *You shouldn't drink spirits at this time of night."* [4]

---

[4] The famous Edward seduction ballad *Have Some Madeira, M'Dear* by Flanders and Swann performed by Lou Gottlieb of *The Limeliters*.

I preferred men, because I wasn't a lesbian, even though I had a lot of sex with women over the years for money. There were times I was tempted to fall in love with a client because I had a genuine connection. It might be good conversation, personality, good looks, good sex, or they were intense in the room; I mean passionate and that's big for me, a huge turn-on and something deeply attractive to me in another person. But I didn't go there, because I had a partner, actually a partner whom I feared.

I had a client who was really good looking, rich, had a beautiful wife and beautiful children, but after their last child, was getting no sex. He used to come in and book me. Even stalked me a bit. But he was married and I would never violate his marriage relationship: the wife, the children. I was there to give him some relief, dissipate his frustration not fall in love with him. He said he had a major crush on me. It was tempting. Very tempting.

So, generally girls strictly avoided falling in love, the clubs rigorously maintained a business separation, and clients were steered away from the inevitable male clinginess which is really just lust. Men often fall in love with prostitutes, they often mistake the service for genuine affection. They're in love with being in love or being loved, or lust.

Clients would 'fall in love' with *Jasmin*, especially because I listened to them. All these clients wanted was to be listened to, treated with respect, desired, valued and wanted. For many men, the only place they could get that was a brothel. That is on many wives. But of course, if they got caught, the men get blamed, and the cycle of toxic finger-pointing continues.

Let me ask the question. If a wife or girlfriend is withdrawing sex, or using sex as a weapon to manipulate or punish her man, what's he supposed to do? Only a saint would be able to endure that, the frustration, enduring celibacy, and remaining faithful to a banshee of a wife. Many good men compensated through a brothel and slept with me, trying to hold on to their marriages and the partners they loved.

I'll say it again. It's not brothels that break up marriages, but affairs.

Clients would ask for my number, what suburb I lived in, what my address was, ask me out. I'd say no or give them false information. I just had to, to maintain professional separation.

When I had regular clients who booked me a lot and we actually got quite close, and they got into the 'friend zone' I'd tell them they needed to book someone else, because it got weird or awkward if you got too close. I didn't want to have sex with friends. I needed separation. Clients who got too close over time got farmed out and I'd disconnect sexually. But I might go and chat with them in the bar at The Club, but never accept a coffee date outside the game. It's just too complicated and threatens your income stream, your career. It was easier for me to have sex with a complete stranger.

But swinging is different. Committed couples start sharing themselves with others and that says to me, there is something missing or askew in their love for one another. The other side is, they could be over-sexed and need that kind of context. I'm ok with that.

I've talked with several veteran sexologists and they all say, that the main thing that ruins relationships is a libido mismatch. Uneven sexual expectations. They should teach this in schools or pre-marriage counseling. I'd encourage all young people to only pick partners with whom they are well-matched sexually, who share a similar libido.

Because of testosterone, men need to get stimulation and nurture their sexual intimacy. They do it to enhance their own relationship, I get that with swingers.

We've all heard of the international bestseller *"Women are from Venus, Men are From Mars."* We are different; we have different languages; different love languages as well. Men offer love to get sex. Women offer sex to get love. As a prostitute I was offering sex for money, to serve or feed the male sexual need or desire; to have sex, so they feel loved.

So, I'd heard about swinging from my Swedish friends, but avoided it. Then I started working.

Male clients can't go to swinging clubs on their own, whereas women can (because men can have sex with several women at once). Males also pay, women don't.

A few months into the job a client wanted to take just me. I was nervous about it, because I didn't know what was there, I didn't know what to do, and all the reasons I've given above about how I felt about swinging.

The client and I rocked up, we were met and given a run down on how it worked and a tour. During the tour we saw people having sex, individually and in groups. It didn't really turn me on because we already had that at work.

We went to the bar and I had about a half dozen cocktails to help me get in to it. While I was at the bar my client had a good voyeuristic tour and got turned on. I never actually had sex with him, he was busy with others; I was his ticket into the swinger's club. I was actually more than happy to sit at the bar and drink while getting paid and avoid the sex activity going on around me. That was my first experience of a swinger's club.

Later, I was often with another girl as a client would book two of us, or more, and we'd all go together to the swinger's club. I usually agreed because it would be an extension, and I would suggest we make it a threesome and he book and take Lily as well, which he did. The swinger's club was only 15 minutes away so Security drove us there with the client.

We arrived and got changed in the locker room just like a public pool, except you go naked, or with the robe you're provided or your own skimpy clothing.

Lily and I stripped and put on the robes as did the client. There is loud music and dimmed lighting so it's difficult to have banter or chat, so we just went through the motions of preparing to have a threesome together. We held his hands and walked him down the corridor. He was a bit drunk, average height, not good looking, about 50, and we led him into the bondage corridor.

At the end, we took his gown off, spun him around roughly and both shackled him up to the brick wall. There were substantial iron shackles bolted to the wall, so we shackled his arms and legs to these in a St Andrew's cross position. There he was, vulnerable and stretched like an 'X'. He just passively let us do that, obviously expecting a lot more. We giggled, turned, and walked away down the corridor and left him there and went to the bar where we kept drinking on his tab.

There was no question of him being ripped off or coming back on us, because anyone in the swinger's club could come along and do whatever they wanted to him; and I'm sure he enjoyed that, which we set up.

We did it as a lark and were always playing practical jokes. We would all have to leave together, you can't just leave a client, so eventually he came back into the bar, naked, and reconnected with Lily and I. He didn't really say anything or tell us off, because he was so drunk. We went back to the locker and all got dressed and headed back to The Club. Security would be there pre-arranged, because the booking is on a clock. Back at The Club, we went and fixed up our makeup, he went off, and Lily and I went back out on the floor to get a new booking.

Another time Jodie and I went to the swinger's club with a client and this time I was shackled up to the wall. The client, Jodie and I were driven there by Security; the client had extended by three hours. I'd persuaded him it would be fun and he'd never tried swinging before. He was quite tantalized and it was an easy extension.

As before, we undressed in the gown room provided. Jodie and I put on the supplied gowns but the client went naked. The three of us proceeded to the bar and drank cocktails for a short while, watching the other couples making out, then Jodie and I suggested we all go to the dungeon area.

There was no-one else there. On the back wall, where the shackles are fixed, are two wooden platforms a few feet above the floor and projecting outward about 20 inches or so. The idea is the 'slave' climbs up on these and stands with legs apart and is then shackled to the wall in a St Andrew's 'X' position.

We were all quite drunk. Jodie suggested I get up and be shackled and have some fun. So I did, took my gown off, climbed up, and Jodie and the client shackled my arms to the wall and I stood there ready for action.

The two of them played with me for a while, it was fleeting, as I wanted to get down. They unshackled me and I stepped down and we got the client up. Jodie and I worked him orally and with our hands till he came. It was quite dark, and he got interested in the group activities going on around us. I went back to the bar until he'd had enough fun and he was ready to go back to The Club.

Some girls like that stuff and specialize in it, and would frequently take clients to swinger's club because they had better facilities than The Club, which was not really a specialist B&D club. Or they'd take privates and indulge clients interested in the same sexuality as they were.

It was a convenient gig down the road and both clubs worked to each others mutual benefit. That might work in a big city where I was, but in other places, swinging goes on in private mansions or rural discreet properties through word of mouth, private invitation or discreet marketing. In my context, the swinger's club was used as an extension of The Club, a variation service available for clients, for which they obviously paid. And we fed 'talent' in to the swingers for them to enjoy in their group sex context. Win-win and the money flowed.

Another time I was there and really out of it on booze and a bit of dope, and I had sex with several men on a huge bed in an orgy. It's actually really dangerous because it's so easy for them to whip their condom off and do you without you knowing because the oil is flowing and you can't always tell. They use a lot of psychedelic music from the sixties and incense. It's all quite hypnotic. The smell, the darkness, candles, the music, it can sweep you into a trance.

It's a big room, separated a bit by partitions and curtains, like a maze. You step up into a room with a bed; step down into a dungeon with the full works; turn a corner and there might be couches where people are making out. It's a playground with beds and couches, platforms, a grope tent, a bird cage, a dungeon.

The grope tent is a small tent suspended from the ceiling. It has hand-sized holes cut out. Whoever goes inside the tent gets groped: tits, balls, cocks, cunts, all get stroked and played with. It's rather fun and very sensual.

I went in to the bird cage a couple of times. It's a huge human-sized old-fashioned bird cage hanging from a chain from the ceiling. I opened the door, stepped inside, held on to the bars, scantily clad, and someone swung me. Perhaps that's where the term comes from. [5] Chicks in bird cages being swung tend to be scantily clad or naked. I tended to wear a short mini skirt at these places, didn't walk around naked although I did once or twice. There was furniture where people had come, so I preferred to have some protection. What I wore was a

---

[5] The term "swinging" (to oscillate or "move freely back and forth") is first known in literature from the mid-sixteenth century. In the mid-1960s during the sexual revolution the phrase was adopted to describe habitual promiscuous sex with multiple partners (for women, especially after the liberation of the pill); to "move about" and enjoy oneself sexually. In 1787 French painter Fragonard painted a sexualized painting for a client of his mistress on a swing while the client gazed up her dress, "The Swing," which may have helped the adoption of the phrase. Playful and erotic scenes such as that were popular amongst European elites in the mid eighteenth century including Fragonard's wealthy patrons. [Editor]

singlet that hung just above my crotch; I wore panties. Guys seemed to like this, as it was a bit sporty. I had been an athlete and had a really athletic body, even now. Tasteful and not over the top – a matching bra and knickers and always quality and sexy in its styling. I like black lacy stuff with a sporting look.

Other girls went with lacy girlie stuff. Girls who wore really over the top stuff tended just to parade around. Some didn't have the figure and it was really 'mutton dressed up as lamb.' But guys like all sorts and types, so there was always variety. But for me, I had a strong sense of my own dignity. I liked it to look 'tight,' attractive, sporty and not sleazy. I certainly attracted a lot of men and got a lot of bookings.

At the orgies, I did 'squirt' once or twice and this became known, so I would be made available as a squirter. I squirted at the orgies not from cock, but from being fingered vigorously. Just a hand doing me. I'd come away never knowing who fingered me so vigorously and made you squirt. It could have been a women for all I knew. And I just added to the feminine cum all over the bed and on everyone else. It was a big turn-on for clients. It also made me a desirable asset at the orgies and it'd get booked for threesomes or foursomes.

Someone tends to oil you up while you're laying on the bed, in preparation for enjoying you. It's not really planned, it just happens and that's what the sex is like. It's a big writhing pile of naked bodies. You just have sex with whatever body is nearby. Best not to look too hard, because the types who go to swinger's clubs tend to be dumpy housewives and middle aged couples. That's why it's dark.

I'd just kiss and stroke and have oral sex (because I like cock) and allow clients (whether men or women) to penetrate me as they wanted and just go with the flow.

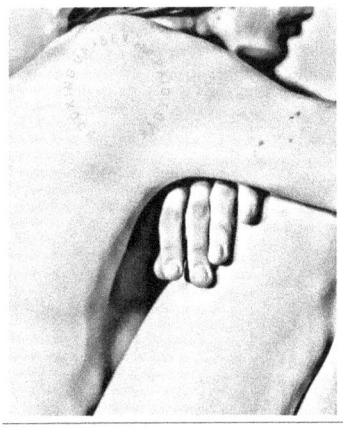

"Intoxication, like sexual euphoria, is the privilege of the human animal. Sexual frenzy is our compensation for the tedious moments we must suffer in the passage of life. "Nothing in excess" professed the ancient Greeks. Why, if I spend half the month in healthy scholarship and pleasant sleep, shouldn't I be allowed the other half to howl at the moon and pillage the groins of Europe's great beauties?"

~ Roman Payne, The Wanderess.

7. Sex, Drugs, Thugs and Hugs

That opening line from the theme song "Married with Children" goes

> "Love and marriage, love and marriage, go together like a horse and carriage..."

With professional sex, Paid Love, "love" is sex and the carriage is drugs.

Drugs are everywhere in the sex trade. They are both defined as vice industries, after all. The predominant drugs I saw, and used, while working were: ecstasy, cocaine and meth. Dope is habitual.

This is because drugs are added value, so both girls, clubs and clients are on the make adding value by selling drugs: to one another, strangers, clients and randoms. On one occasion a client couldn't pay and offered me a huge bag of dope.

"I don't smoke that s**t" I said, but I took it nevertheless, made lots of reefers using roll your owns, and sold them for $100 a piece to clients. Usually they were $10, but when a client is drunk, he doesn't mind. For many, money is no object, $1000 is the same as $10, and if they'd baulk, I'd say *"don't take it then,"* and not take their booking. So, they'd buy the dope at an exorbitant price, as well as the booking, to get me.

Cocaine was the main drug, but it doesn't last and only gives you a slight elevated high. Personally, I don't see what people see in it. Meth, or 'P,' affects people in different ways, usually very badly. It's very addictive. Users can cope for a few months and then suddenly become addicted. It's all down hill from there. I've seen lawyers, wealthy businessmen, beautiful girls, just ruined in months by meth. They can lose everything: yachts, businesses, marriages, families, friends, and everything they own. It's a huge price to pay for a temporary elevated state.

I tried meth once, went with a guy and we smoked $2000 worth at his place. I wasn't getting an effect, so we lit up and smoked more and more in a glass pipe, heating the crystal meth till it melts and the fumes are what you draw back in to your lungs. We thought we'd been smoking for an hour, but it was eight. Under meth, time just flys past but you don't, like in Narnia.

The only effect I got was a really pounding heart and a sore chest. I also got a clenched jaw and didn't sleep for three days. I never got a high, so that was it for me, I never tried it again.

Others had different experiences; euphoric, which is why it's so popular. They feel invincible but the drug makes them delusional. For us working girls, meth made the clients feel like they were hard. But they weren't. I saw some really bizarre stuff. It also catalyses a lot of violence; much of the hideous crime we see in society today is meth-induced.

Meth-users pull weird faces and behave oddly and can be unpredictable. The girls often got massive abscesses and lost their teeth. Meth seems to affect women worse than men. But it still rots their teeth and makes them crazy. They lose weight, get really spotty.

A girl came in once, she was new, stick thin, eyes bulging (another symptom of meth), just staring and clicking her fingers uncontrollably like some weird stick insect.

Another time a client just went nuts and kicked in one of the room doors. There were people in there having a good time and he couldn't get in, so kicked his way in thinking he was somewhere else.

It would also make guys attempt to spike girls' drinks. Clients would often behave oddly like you would in a virtual reality game. That's effectively what meth does, it alters people's mindsets and they are in a fantasy bubble, a virtual reality. That's why it's so dangerous. And for those of us looking on, it can be absurd, scary, weird. It also takes a terrible toll physically, especially on slight petite girls. We've all seen the photos of a meth-head before, after, and at the end.

My drug of choice was ecstasy. In my working days, it was more pure, so it was much better and less harmful than today. Nowadays people are greedy, so you're ingesting rat poison, powdered sleeping tablets, all sorts of chemical compounds ground together to max-out the ecstasy. The concoction can be lethal and often is. I saw many girls go to the hospital.

Meth prevents erection, so is terrible for workers who might have to blow or handjob for ages. The client feels he's erect and hot like a prize stud, but physically it's not happening which is exhausting for a working girl. Trying to blowjob or be screwed by a flaccid penis is like eating peas with chopsticks.

Unlike meth, ecstasy makes people feel really sensual and uninhibited and they stay sexual for three or four hours. But try maintaining an erection for three hours. So men often take ecstasy in conjunction with viagra so their body keeps up with their mind. Ecstasy for the mind, viagra for the erection.

This is great for women. I can enjoy sexual and sensual pleasure with a man for three or four hours. Female feelings stay the same, but men became flaccid, so ecstasy actually enhances sex, because you can maintain the experience for hours especially with viagra. It simply prolongs the ability to make love.

But as a private love-making tool, especially for impotence, viagra is a great chemical - and mostly harmless, it simply increases blood flow for men. Viagra makes men rock hard, but for up to twelve hours so it has to be managed.

I took viagra once to see what it would do. Effect? Nothing at all. Viagra is strictly a male drug although female viagra is apparently manufactured.

It was obvious most male clients took it before they came to The Club, as they were always erect when they arrived and tended to stay that way.

Ecstasy can ruin sex. After you've had it several times, sex just isn't as good without it, so your relationship is controlled by the need to take ecstasy. And as I said, ecstasy is now full of shit, it's poisonous.

It was a girl's birthday and her client had heaps of meth, she had a little. He was out of it, and after she had smoked hers she piped up on his and the room was filled with meth, which has a horrible chalky smell and taste, stings your eyes, and fills the room with a white mist. He'd booked her and me, so I sat there with a towel over my head trying not to inhale all the meth smoke. When he came to, he was furious. He told her off and made her pay him for the meth she'd smoked. I left the room.

Later she got a massive abscess under her armpit, the size of a tennis ball. I remember going to the kitchen and she was on the floor crying and showed me the abscess. I called one of the managers and Security took her to hospital for treatment. She was on a drip for three days.

People are in a brothel for similar reasons they are on drugs, thus "horse and carriage." They're blocking or hiding from something or seeking surrogacy from real life and avoiding problems. For a moment, while on a drug (like booze) or having sex with a stranger, a hooker, you can forget yourself, your issues. The mundanity of life slips away like an outgoing tide and you can feel wanted, desired, appreciated (as long as you pay).

Obviously drugs attract controllers in to the industry, and gangs are like brothel wallpaper. They muscle in and try to monopolize to maximize profits; get girls hooked and gangs manipulate them as client-suppliers. Or take them over and pimp them out, themselves.

Gangsters would come and book girls to sell drugs to them, whether dope, cocaine, meth. It wouldn't even be about sex, just selling drugs. The Club was a gangsters' paradise. Easy girls, easy money, easy deals and because many of them are socially inept, and even struggle to hold adult conversations or relate to women, easy sex. For the most part, they were respectful and easy clients. Like most men, they just wanted the attention.

I didn't have that many gangsters as clients; mainly they where in to try and hook girls in as drug users or pushers, and because I avoided that, I didn't connect with them as much as I could have. As men, they were relatively clean, because they were loaded. They wore gold watches and necklaces but had to take their patches off at the door so they would't fight inside. The Club had to remain a neutral place. Also, some of the girls were scared of them, so the patches stayed at the door.

Workers and clients habitually smoked dope. I smoked a little, but I hit a bad batch and it made us all ill, synthetic dope it was. That put me off, and dope never really featured in my sex work except as a product I on-sold and made money from.

I'd get my dope mainly from other girls. I also had friends who grew it.

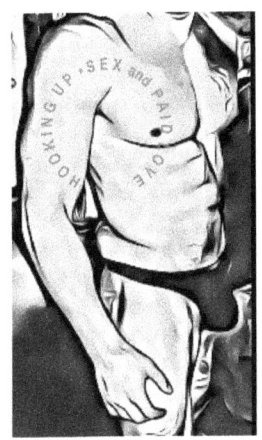

"Хуем груши околачивать."

~ *Russian vulgarism.*

8. Vodka and Caviar

One of my favorite clients was a tall good looking Russian called Sasha. He was 6ft 5," well built, had an air of sophistication and confidence. He had loads of money, maybe Russian mafia money, corrupt fishing money, oligarchy dividends or maybe he was just a smart businessman. Despite all that, he was very nice.

He came in to The Club, looked around all the girls, spotted an empty seat by me, and sat down.

I nervously said

"Hi, I'm Jasmin."

"I was about to walk out the door, then I spotted you," he said. Good start Russkie!

"You look different from the other girls. You look more sophisticated." (older?). I was flattered.

We didn't talk long and he invited me back to his place. The manager said there wasn't a car available as Security were all out on escort duty. He offered to take me in his car, which the manager was iffy about as it was a safety issue. She asked me if I was happy to do that. They let me do quite a few things they'd never let the younger girls do, because I was confident and could handle myself, at least in their eyes.

He booked me for eight hours and we went off in his car. It was an old classic Mercedes. We chatted on the way to his place, about a 20 minute drive, about anything and nothing.

Pulling up, his home was a double story townhouse, nothing flash. We parked up and went inside. He wined me and we chatted a lot first. I was embarrassed as I'd had vaginitis which is a bacterial infection you can get from rough sex and I'd had a rough patch the week or so before.

My doctor had given me really strong antibiotics to clear it. You can still work, as it's not contagious, and the drugs knock out the smell vaginitis has, pretty quickly. But you can't drink. And I forgot. I was knocking back champagne with Sasha.

I had to go to the loo and threw up, a reaction to the drugs. I told him I was on antibiotics (not about the vaginitis) and had just had a reaction. After I'd thrown up, I felt ok, I just had to stop drinking.

We went to the bedroom and had sex. He was quite intense but the sex was good. I mean physically, not like the tradesmen who just 'bang bang bang' you, there was a connection. He seemed to respect me, almost like being with a boyfriend. Maybe that's why I enjoyed the sex. I felt it was really good, satisfying. He had a nice body, tall, big cock, but gentle and caring and that makes the sex good, meaningful. If more guys understood this about women, sex could be so much more meaningful for both partners. Men need to get past their testosterone lust, the banging, and reach inside women's psyches and their needs.

This is the difference with prostitution and clubs. They are lust factories, just servicing male testosterone-drive, male desire. Women are getting money in exchange, not good sex, emotional satisfaction or fulfillment physically. But occasionally, some of us loved the sex if we hit a special client who was more mindful and pleasant, thoughtful and emotional outside himself, balanced his selfish sexual needs. I met a few clients like that, but they were few and far between.

Sasha and I had sex then slept. Eight hours later the time was up. I was collected by Security and driven back to The Club as the sun came up. A good night financially, and fun.

He came in the next night and booked me again, for a 12 hour escort back to his place. Seafood dinner with some young male businessmen colleagues he appeared to be mentoring or something. We sat round having dinner at his place, me and three men.

We were drunk and fell asleep, so I slept half the booking. We had sex in the morning. I loved the sleeping bookings, best hourly rate in the world, and I didn't have to sleep when I got home, could get on with a life during the day. Where else can you get paid to sleep and then go home and enjoy their money?

After that, he come in to The Club fairly regularly and always booked me. We'd go out to eat, drink, then he'd extend.

A few days later, he was back again. The girls flocked to the bar because by now, word was around he was a big booker. He booked me ten hours and extended me another four as well as booking Angela who thought of herself as a bit of a kingpin in the game.

Angela was a fat buxom chick who'd been on the game twenty years or more. She felt superior to all the other girls, they'd all bow down, except me, I didn't bow down to anyone unless they were paying. I bowed down to money. He booked Angela ten hours and me 14 hours together and took us to the supermarket.

He bought seafood, loads of champagne, and we went back to his place, that two story town house. We talked most of the night and Sasha got annoyed with Angela for always being on her phone, texting and not including him in conversation.

Sasha had intended to have anal with both of us that night, thus the double booking, each of us one after the other. I made out I'd never done it before, that I was an 'anal virgin' and wasn't keen to do it. The truth was, I'd had a bit of anal, maybe once or twice and only with boyfriends, never in The Club, so in a way I was sort of an anal virgin (I'd not done it in The Club because I didn't like it and I certainly wasn't going to do it for $200 like Angela). So I played up and Sasha payed up. That really pissed Angela off. I was getting ten times what she'd got earlier for anal sex. She sulked and started begging and griping and tried to negotiate.

Sasha took us both on his lounge floor right there, doggy-style. He took me first, obviously wanting me more as an 'anal virgin' and I played that up, pretending it was really sore and hard (he had a large cock, so it was actually quite sore and he was certainly hard). I hadn't done it that much, as I said. Anuses need to stretch slowly over time, not like vaginas that are more elastic. The muscles are also designed to push out, so you're going against the natural flow of what an anus is designed for. It's designed to push things out, not have things pushed in, unlike the vagina which is mostly made for sex and babies.

Sasha is doing me anally on the lounge floor and I'm playing along as a supposed virgin, which in turn turned him on, hard. It didn't last long, maybe a minute (best $2000 I ever made) because I was wincing and 'aah-ing' a lot, as if it was hurting. He pulled his cock out, removed the condom, put a new condom on his erect penis and thrust into Angela who didn't squeal - a seasoned anal receptacle.

I sat and had a cigarette and watched Sasha bang the queen on all fours that I 'd just dethroned.

He pulls out, and that was the the end of that. Angela really on the back foot.

She left and was picked up. I slept with him, literally. Another four hours we woke up. He asked for a blow job, he came in my mouth with a condom, and that was it. He then took me in to town for shopping, so another extension past the 14 hours. We went to a brand store and he spent $2600 on clothes for me: a beautiful suede jacket, nice tops, beautiful high grey ankle boots, really nice trousers, expensive sunglasses and a hand bag. I felt like a million dollars because I went back to work and the day shift girls went "wow!"

I wrote at the time, "*I think he really really likes me.*"

He came in a few weeks later but I was already booked. So he booked some other girls until I was free and I joined him later for whatever time was left.

The last time I saw him was a few weeks later. He booked me and four other girls and took us all off to a room upstairs. He made us all drink whiskey straight, on the rocks. Then he made us all lie on the bed with our legs apart and g-strings off, like sardines. Didn't bother me, felt like a fun game, I was up for it.

Sasha went along the line and fingered everyone to see who was wet. One girl was dry, probably because she was on meth and he kicked her out. She was also stupid, because we all knew to quickly lube up before a booking so we looked like we were wet for the client, excited by them and ready to receive cock.

We were annoyed. She got kicked out, still got paid and could go off and book another client while we all had to 'work.' Pissed us all off no-end. But we all laughed about it and with the girl, afterward. She was so embarrassed but it was hilarious.

Sasha had been in a bad mood that night, when he lined us all up, a dominance thing I expect. One man over several women. Looking back, I think he was under stress and was worried. He was leaving for Russia two days later and perhaps he was scared. He'd talked to me a little about some of his heavy contacts and some of the stuff he was in to. I never pried. Didn't want to know, to be honest.

We'd all had so many whiskies including Sasha, there was a bit of sex and I remember he took me hard and rough on the bed, as if he knew he'd not see me again.

I liked him because he'd often pay for an overnighter. We'd go to bed, snuggle, he'd fall asleep, as I would, and I'd get paid per hour for sleeping. He didn't mind at all, seemed to like paying extravagantly for nice company, and I was. We'd talk.

He tried to book me privately a bit; even asked me to move in while he was away in Russia and he'd pay me $2000 a week to care for his aging mother. But that was a restriction. I could earn more at The Club and didn't fancy washing and caring for an elderly mother. Too convenient for him. Offended my sense of independence and self determination. And besides, it was all too domestic.

That was the last time I ever saw him.

I was sad. He said he had some loose ends to tie up in Moscow and was in danger; nonchalantly told me he was under threat and might not come back. I never heard from him again.

The sex was good though. I like tall strong men. They envelope me in their masculinity and I feel safe. Stupid I know, sleeping as a hooker with a Russian oligarch under threat with gangsters next door selling P. But you can't extract the humanity from these bizarre pantomimes we all live. People are still people. We all want the same thing —to be loved. And a big strong guy with a sexy Russian accent with his arms wrapped around me, paying me a lot of money each night, sounds good to me.

It was. I have sexy high ankle boots to prove it.

"The differences that separate
human beings are
nothing compared to the
similarities that bond us together."

~ Sophie Gregoire Trudeau.

9. Gays, Lesbians and Trans

After I joined The Club, and found I was actually making love to women on occasions, either one-on-one, couples, or as a bi-girl for a client, I decided to pop round and see my lesbian friends Rosie and Alle.

I asked them about the lesbian scene because I wanted to know. I was curious to expand my knowledge in a casual way because I'd been booked by a woman, actually a couple. The couple were middle-aged, a bit boring, and had booked two girls. I was one and was selected for the lady. She lay on her stomach and I gave her a sensual massage which included fingering her. She wriggled around a bit, moaning and groaning but there wasn't much to it. The husband got the same with the other girl and a bit of a hand job. So, I was interested to learn more from Rosie and Alle what they liked, how their relationship worked, and what went on in their bedroom.

Rosie and Alle taught me more about lesbian interaction in everyday life and a bit about lesbian love-making "tongue in groove" as we and they called it. They were a bit embarrassed and not that forthcoming.

When you're in the game, you get pretty callous and indifferent to sex and it's extreme forms and can forget that others are not as acculturated as you are. Quite a few times in my diary I noticed I'd written something like, *"once again, the abnormal has become normal."* I was on a slippery slope of creeping abnormality.

It's different for all lesbians. They tend not to like cock for various seasons, yet some mimic heterosexual sexuality by pegging one another with a strap-on (either conventionally or anally). Lesbian sex is as varied as non-lesbian sex. Human sexuality is varied. It's fluid.

I was booked by another couple, a really wild couple, and escorted to their house. They were in their late thirties, high as kites, music up loud. It was 4am in the morning. I came in. They were naked in the lounge. They gave me some alcohol and it was just full-on threesome sex: him banging me, her going down on me, me going down on her; kind of like being accosted. A big drunken blur really. I enjoyed it, maybe an hour or two but after I went back to The Club, I grabbed a spare room and slept, as I couldn't drive home intoxicated.

The couple were very nice. We talked a little but the booking ended, the driver arrived, and I departed, just business sex as usual. A fun out-there hippy couple.

Two lesbian girls worked at The Club, not especially for lesbian clients, just whatever, like I did as a heterosexual.

But they didn't last long. They didn't like cock. Go figure! You're working a brothel and have issues with cock? Bit like a vegetarian working in an abattoir.

"Trannies" —men dressed as women, drag, cross dressers and men who've had their breasts done (transgender are different) —would sometimes come in wanting attention: drinks, chatting, a bit of fun with some girls; mainly kissing and wanking, rarely intercourse, because it usurps their attempt at female persona and undermines what they're trying to say, do and be.

We had a shy but colorful 'mascot' at The Club. Roland was a young cross dresser and would come in with frills flappin', high heels and makeup melting off him. He really looked the part but was really humble. He never had any money so never booked girls but he'd hang out with us, chat; we all liked him and tolerated him more than the other Barflies.

The transgender clients were women or men who have surgically or culturally changed their gender, that is, they self-identify differently to their biology or have had surgery to actually modify their biology. They are quite different than a cross-dresser, like Eddie Izzard the actor and comedian.

It's a broad definition that is quite fluid. In my context, a "transgender" is a human being assigned a different gender than they had at birth, such as on their birth certificate, based on their biological genitalia. And a person who has changed their gender medically (with drugs, ie testosterone and steroids, among others) to "become" the other gender, or have had surgery to mimic the opposite gender. But I'm not interested in all that political debate; it'll settle down in a decade or two as society recognizes the semantics of it all, the way the majority does with most things like "gay" and "queer" which oscillated for quite a while as defined terms.

The Trans ("woman") working girls would want to book a man, and have sex with a man to reiterate their "womanhood." One Trans 'girl' I worked with was from Thailand, absolutely beautiful. She'd had the full sex change, that is, s/he had breasts and a vagina created, where there'd originally been a penis.

The Club was obligated to explain this to a client. Maria lost a lot of bookings because of this. I felt sorry for 'her,' as 'she' was lovely, but men rejected 'her' because 'she'd' once been a guy who'd changed. The clients she did go with didn't mind, and were even turned on by the fact they were fucking a guy who was now a woman. Others liked that it was both/and or just the exoticness of it all.

I got Maria a booking once with a regular client, as a threesome. He was curious. And so was I. Her surgery was amazing. You would never know and she enthusiastically showed off her vagina. They had another hour together. I was happy to help her make some money and she deserved it.

Trans clients would also come in, that is, guys who are now females, wanting sex with women, technically lesbianism, but with a male backstory. They might want regular sex with their modified vagina or anal. Or any of the extras on offer. This was rare, mainly they'd just work as prostitutes.

Gay guys would come in too, maybe if there was a parade on, have drinks, but I never saw them book or have sex. There were always bi-sexual people and obviously people were enjoying threesomes and foursomes, or swinging elsewhere, but that is not really "gay" as such. It's all a bit of an alphabet soup: LGBTQi+ (the "+" is QP2SAA). [6]

---

[6] Lesbian, gay, bisexual, transgender, queer, intersex… +questioning, pansexual, two-spirit (2S), androgynous and asexual. The two Qs are often put together. LGBTQQIP2SAA (Editor).

Personally I think its silly to try and categorize people according to their sexuality, as human sexuality is fluid and changes. But because it was about "human" rights, well the gay community especially, and women before them, the arguments did a lot to categorize a "community" based on sexual practice. And Trans are trying (and struggling) to follow suit. It'll sort itself out. There's so much more to being human than how you have sex.

A queer sex worker in Australia who started at 19 wrote a novel about her experiences when she was 26. She said she now hardly has sex in her private life.

> *"[I'm] far more celibate than people expect me to be in my private life, and purely interested in sex within emotional connection..."* [7]

---

[7] "Tilly Lawless: 'I became a sex worker to help me through university,'" Sydney Morning Herald, 22 August 2021.

A guy came and took a bit of an interest in me. He was dressed really gay, had a beautiful home, booked me for a private but just cooked for me, for several hours and we chatted the whole night. He came in a few times, booked me but we never had sex and then he started booking other girls. Maybe he just wanted some female company as a gay man.

I had a regular cross dresser called Robyn. He would come in already dressed and liked to sit and chat and go out for dinner. He was a little old man with a beard shadow dressed in women's clothing, fish net stockings and high heels and really nicely painted nails, but was obviously a man. So, going out for dinner was a bit embarrassing. We we went to really nice places; it was a booking, so I didn't mind, and he was actually very nice. We had sex once, regular intercourse, but he'd usually book two girls and I'd let the other girl do him and I'd sit there and chat with him.

Bizarre I know, there he is on his back with a girl doing him cowboy style, and his head is turned to the side chatting to naked ol' me sitting on the side of the bed chatting back.

You have to realize, that in the game, sex becomes really mundane with clients and girls, and is just par for the course. You become desensitized. Sitting watching two people have sex can be like watching people drink tea, if you're doing and watching it several times a night, five days a week, for several years.

A business guy took me on a booking to his home in the city and gave me some clothes to wear. These included some kinky lingerie and some panties that his previous girlfriend had worn, unwashed. I refused to wear those.

He came out of his room, cross-dressed. I was shocked. He took loads of 'rush' up his nose. [8] It gave him red watery eyes and it looked like his head was going to explode. But it apparently gave him heightened sexual desire. He liked to sit in the chair opposite me and wanted me to masturbate in bed wearing his girlfriends panties. I reluctantly wore them over the top of mine. I thought it was sick weirdo stuff.

Prostitutes were often surrogates for broken relationships and clients would want you to pretend to be them, look like them, so they could fantasize about having sex with the person they still loved and had lost. It's an important and valuable service Paid Love workers provide people who are broken and lonely and missing someone that was there for them. It's a way of maintaining the connection, like those people who keep their dead

---

[8] "Rush" a colloquialism for amyl nitrate which causes blood vessels to dilate lowering blood pressure and relaxing muscles. Inhaled directly from a bottle it is used to enhance sexual experiences, commonly by gay men or as a party drug. [Editor].

parents 'alive' mummified in a room for years, serial killers who keep 'trophies,' or those ancient cultures who buried their ancestors under the floors of their houses to keep them present.

Another guy booked me, oiled me up, and we body slid on each other while he referred to me as "Mary Sue" an ex-girlfriend. So I was obviously the body double. There was a lot of that sort of thing.

We had a tall and beautiful hooker called Jane who preferred to socialize and was rather picky with her clients. A particular client she didn't like, was pestering her to book and she ignored him, until finally she gave in. As he went to pay she rubbed herself up against him and whispered in his ear, *"I can't wait to show you my cock!"* His eyes bulged and he ran for the exit. Her plan worked, to get rid of him. We all laughed in the bar.

"I have built so many boats of love,
but they will never touch water
and they will never reach you."

~ Amrutha.

10. Sports, Scoring and Love Boats

Sports and Balls

I was a successful athlete and had a trim body. This got me a lot of bookings. Successful sportsmen have a lot of testosterone and they almost inevitably have a strong sex drive (and usually a strong ego). A lot of well known sports people and celebrities came in to The Club.

I've fucked a lot of well-known guys. I'll never disclose their names, but I had plenty. It was fun, flattering. Some of them were terrible; others were great lovers.

Celebrity sportsmen tended to come in through the discrete back door. There was no nondisclosure agreement, it was just a given that you wouldn't talk about your clients; an unspoken rule. What goes on in The Club, stays in The Club. Otherwise, clients won't come and girls won't get paid.

I had a regular client, a well known sportsmen but he had this thing where he always liked to come on my face, never inside me. I didn't like that, it felt disrespectful, degrading. He'd stand back, and spray. It was messy, and remember, I had to clean up afterwards, and it required a total reapplication of my makeup.

I could never work out why he came to book a hooker, as he always talked about his girlfriend, how happy they were. But he'd come most weeks and always booked me, so clearly he wasn't that happy, or was sexually mismatched and needed release, a top-up, or might have been a sex addict. Some guys are just too much for their girlfriends.

Girls were always well made up. Nails had to be done, good hair, tasteful heavy makeup, well done. In the same way that a shorter skirt works at The Club, eyelash extensions, brows manicured, waxed legs, waxed fanny, asshole bleached, it's all extreme in this game. It's about attracting clients from the lounge, amongst a school of 20-25 feeding females, so it's strong competition for who gets the money.

A lot of girls had breast implants, 'bolt-ons' we called them. Others had buttock implants. I tended to exercise to keep the shape I wanted. It worked, until it didn't.

An international Asian sportsmen came in to The Club. Usually they like the young girls, but he kept starring at me. He came over and grabbed my arm, pulled me up off the couch and we went to a room. We sort of played around a bit, kissing, fondling, hugging, then he said he wanted to take me back to his hotel. So he booked me for ten hours. It was early, so we went and had dinner.

Later, up in his room, masturbating one another, we had sex and chatted about his sport, the international circuit. And we slept. He was nice. He wanted me to come on tour with him, but I said no. It would have been the end of my job. I had to balance two weeks really well paid work with income over the next several years. Those gigs never panned out, in that sense. The sex was ok, some Asians can be a bit rough, a bit disrespectful, not as disrespectful as other cultures, though.

Before departing the booking at 6am, I pulled back the hotel curtains, and found a huge cruise liner had pulled in beside the dockside hotel during the night. There I was completely starkers and all these cruise guests looking straight in to the hotel room at me. I actually took a photo, it was hilarious. I did a bit of a dance for them and pulled the curtains closed again.

Another sportsmen invited me to come on an extended cruise over Christmas with him. He really wanted me to come and be his escort. He showed me the brochures, it looked amazing, all expenses paid. But again, he'd be shagging me all night, every night, and I wouldn't get paid. And being away from The Club, it's actually going backwards, as glamorous and fun as it seems. Young girls got hoodwinked by the invitations. It's very flattering and can make you feel special. But us older chicks were a bit wiser about the long term.

Sometimes I might pretty annoyed with a client if he was arrogant or rude.Sometimes they think they own your body and can do whatever they want with you. It's a service not a commodity-purchase. I'd buzz down for the condoms and ask really loudly over the intercom so everyone in the bar could hear,

"Can you send up the smallest condoms we have!"

Bit of an inside joke amongst the girls to do that. The client would go all mousey and there'd be no more trouble from him.

As well as celebrity sportsmen, I had well-known actors and singers as clients as well.

The Love Boats: Yachts and Launches, 'Gin Palaces'

A young guy, addicted to meth, was working as deck crew on a luxury three-masted yacht, long and sleek, about 90m long. He was deck crew. He booked me back to the yacht after several hours in The Club, but he couldn't come because he was on meth.

I'm not sure how he got me on board or why an expensive yacht like that was not crewed at the time. We went down into a cabin and had sex on one of the master suit beds. He was able to come at that point. It was *"Wham-Bam-Thank-You-Mam"* and I got up and left. I had to call Security to come early and pick me up. It was fun, though, to be on a yacht like that, see what it was like inside, and have sex in such an opulent environment. But the client wasn't much chop.

There were the sleek long racing yachts like I was on, and then the smaller luxury launches - or "gin palaces" as we called them - about 25m long that frequent big city harbors. Size is all important.

I got booked on both at various stages.

A group of us got booked on to a "gin palace" by a group of guys, me and five other girls. Security dropped us off at the boats and we went on board with our clients. The music went up, the booze flowed and the girls were dancing and doing strip tease.

But I had to sit beside the captain who was a bit stern. I wanted to get up and dance and play but had to sit with him and watch, like a king and queen.

There was a yacht next door with young guys on it watching and laughing and the girls kept inviting them to come over. The clients got horny and wanted sex so the couples went off to their respective cabins and got it on. I went with mine, the captain. He was a bit intense to have sex with, a bit serious, but we still got it on and he seemed happy. He wanted me to stay the rest of the night, so he extended another ten hours, but all the other girls went back to The Club.

We slept, had sex in the morning, he cooked breakfast in the galley, bacon and eggs, and then all the boys and I piled into someone's car. We didn't all fit, so I had to sit on someone's knee. A free lap dance? It was all good humored and we were all laughing and they dropped me back at The Club.

The captain booked me a few times after that. It never got better, he was always serious, but it was a booking I enjoyed because I going out onto a launch and having sex on the boat, which was different and fun.

I had a regular Scottish client, a successful manager in construction. His mate had a big luxury launch and he booked me as an escort on to it with two other girls because there were two others guys on the boat, so one girl for each guy.

This was a ring-in so we met the client down on the dock and went up on to the launch after Security had checked everything. We drank lots of alcohol, smoked lots of dope, and had sex with our clients in the boat's lounge, altogether.

It's was mainly me having the sex as the other men with their girls just kept on talking and dancing. My client decided to strip me in front of everyone, which I didn't enjoy, but was too drunk to care. He then fucked me on the bar in front of everyone, but they were all so drunk they probably didn't even notice, or care.

The boys wanted to extend, but the owner didn't. I think he wasn't having such a good time with his girl, so the booking ended and Security came and we three girls left and went back to The Club.

But the Scot kept coming and booking me. I never went back to the launch, he just came to The Club and booked me there.

Late one morning about 5am, I came into The Club from a hard escort job with a regular client. I was exhausted and looking forward to going home to sleep. The manager greeted me at the door saying,

> "Thank God you're here. I have a client in a room with one girl but he wants another."

All the other girls were booked. I reluctantly agreed and went to the room to meet him. He was a business man from overseas and had paid for two hours. As I stripped to get into the shower, he said, *"Let's go back to my hotel instead."*

We went to the office to organize a driver and payment and he booked the two of us for another ten hours. We were driven to a flash city hotel, but he left for work meetings, said he'd be back at 5pm. So, we slept, went for lunch and had a massage at the hotel spa on his tab. On his return he wanted to book another 12 hours. The other girl wanted to go home. I thought that was a bit odd for such an easy and well paid booking. You don't give up bookings like that. Something about needing to feed her cat. Expensive cat food!

I called a partner in crime to hurry into work because I had a big booking lined up for her (I usually worked with her on threesomes). She eventually arrived and payment was sorted while 'cat-girl' disappeared.

Wow, what a night that was. We hit the booze in the hotel room, ordered room service and lavishly ordered loads of food. Then later that evening we left for the city centre where we hit up the strip clubs. So much fun. The client booked a private room with a pole dancer and loads of alcohol. The pole dancer was a bit young and nervous. The client got bored and left. We stayed with the girl saying,

> "Don't worry about dancing. Just sit and chat and drink with us."

She was so sweet and happy to still be on the clock.

When her hour was up, we left the room to go find our client. He was busy at the main stage placing endless bank notes into girls' lingerie. He was rotten drunk by this stage. We called a cab and he came back with us to the hotel. It was about 2am.

There was still no sex involved that night. He woke to go to business meetings again and we got picked up to go back to The Club. Our long booking was over.

But he booked us the next night, privately, again for 12 hours, and the fun continued: eating at swanky restaurants and getting spa treatments during the day again all on his account while he was at his business meetings.

That evening when he finished up his work obligations, we went for a nice dinner out at a very posh waterfront restaurant, eventually retiring to the hotel reasonably early. The client was exhausted and then the phone calls from his wife began…from overseas!! There was screaming on the end of the line as she demanded to know where all the money was going from their bank account.

It was a bit embarrassing and I didn't know whether to feel sorry for her or our generous client.

Eventually he had sex with me and my work partner, one after the other. A bit half ass'ed as we were all tired from lack of sleep. I let my girl finish him off as I watched TV on the couch in the early hours of the morning trying to stay awake. He left to go back overseas that day. He gave me a beautiful bottle of perfume that was meant for his secretary.

I never saw him again.

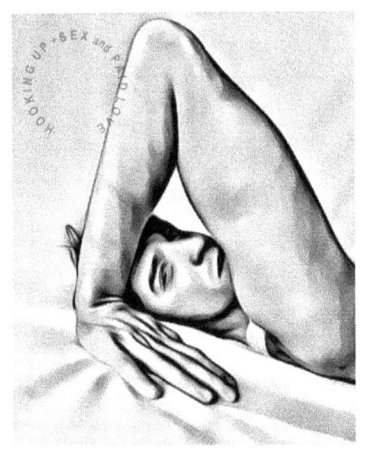

"Work is the refuge of people who have nothing better to do."

~ Oscar Wilde.

11. Mixing Work and Pleasure

One of the problems of working in a big city, is that I'd been an employee as well as an employer in the city. On rare occasions ex-staff or bosses or ex-colleagues could turn up at The Club. This is a problem because people talk, like the Insurance rep. who turned up, and he's going to go back and tell the entire insurance industry I'm working at The Club, isn't he?

You can imagine, the next day, he could tell all my ex employees about what I was now doing, and their families, and it just creates ripples of problems amongst your community of interest outside work.

An ex-employee of mine, a chef, came in. I came back from an escort and he was at the lounge bar. I had to pass him to get to the office to get my escort money. As I walked past I recognized him. I was surrounded by mirrors and I noticed he was looking at me, his ex boss. I told the manager,

> *"I'm not turning around, because that guy is an ex employee."*

I asked her to distract him so I could get away, but he was actually so drunk, he just put his head on the bar and probably wouldn't remember anything.

There was another guy I'd been closely associated with previously in business. I'd worked for him. He'd actually nearly bought one of my partner and my businesses. He had a reputation amongst the girls for being rough - a real 'banger,' slapping, pushing girls around. He came in to The Club.

I avoided him, but he kept staring at me. I'd always leave the room until he was booked. So, that cramped my style quite a bit.

Another ex colleague I'd worked with in insurance, rang me and said,

> "Hey X I hear you're working at The Club. Can we get together for a private?" I said,

> "No Richard, I can't, I don't want to mix work and friendship."

Richard only rang me because another ex-colleague from the same company, Sean, had come in and tried to book me and I'd refused. Sean had already paid for me, so I had to convince him to go with someone else. I think perhaps he wanted to see if I'd go with Richard, having refused him. Ego-games.

If you let your sex work cross over in to your private life, apart from your partner knowing (which they should; keeping a lie like that throughout your whole relationship is underlaying dishonesty and 'cheating') it can ruin all your friendships or affect your circle of interests. And that can be really isolating and damaging to your wider life.

It's absolutely important, if you're going to be a sex worker, to keep the job on the job, and well away from the rest of your life. Because not everyone can deal with it. And you inevitably get judged. There is prejudice and your whole personhood gets defined as a prostitute, a loose women, someone with no morals. Any guys you worked with or were genuine mates with, start coming on to you, hoping for free sex. Because if you're a prostitute, well then, you're just a 'horn bag' and are up for anything, aren't you? To the contrary, as I discussed with *Government Benefits*, it's a job you pay tax on (if you choose to).

On tax, *Government Benefit's* had notices up in The Club about paying tax. But in reality, they turned a blind eye and let us work tax free. I think that's because it's a bit embarrassing if the Government was earning money (tax) from girls selling their bodies for sex. Government as pimp via taxes. Not a good look.

I had a reasonably regular client who lost his wife. He was a sad older gentleman, absolutely loaded, and he'd book me for long bookings at The Club, like 12 hours usually with another girl. It seemed like he wanted to experiment a bit, perhaps doing things he'd never done with his wife: wanted women to sleep with, have sex, try a bit of anal, try a few other things that maybe he'd fantasized about. He was sad and I think he was trying to reconnect with his wife. We just played along and serviced his needs as best we could.

A lovely regular client I had was an excellent guitarist and had toured with several big names before they became famous. He'd bring his guitar in and just serenade me in the room and other girls. He played me some of their new songs that later became really famous with those musicians. That was pretty cool. He also didn't usually have sex, just liked to play and have company.

I really liked some of the girls and several of us got on, especially if I was working men with them (and we were therefore not competition with one another, but were helping one another out as a twosome booking threesomes and foursomes). We'd became friends. I'm still in touch with some of them and I'd invite some to my home for dinner and we'd talk about work and clients. Some of these girls went on to have successful professional careers in legitimate industries. They're doing all sorts of cool things now and have left the Paid Love game behind. It was just a way to fund their studies or get started financially. I worked with all sorts of women: nurses, university students, housewives, mothers, hairdressers, lots of solo mums, anybody really. Prostitutes come from all walks of life. As do clients.

I had a client who owned a business. Gerry would come in regularly and he'd bring all his male employees in regularly as well, for birthdays or other special occasions like someone leaving the firm. He'd shout them a two hour booking each and always book me, but for a longer time. The trouble was, his employees would finish and start knocking on his door saying can we extend for another hour, so our booking was always interrupted. I've said earlier, that was always a good thing, it would extend a booking or use up time. But I liked this client and we might be deep in conversation about something. There was also the risk he might book another girl himself and my eight-hour booking might truncate to two or four hours. He'd book me until he ran out of money, so I wanted him to fly solo with me, not insert other girls in on my gig, while he was inserting himself in to me!

He was really lovely and I had a bit of a crush on him because we connected. It would take him ages to come which was a pain. He was also really cocky and self assured, bordering on arrogance or obnoxiousness. I hated it but liked it at the same time; I was attracted to that.

Other girls really disliked him, saying he treated them badly. He never treated me that way and was always respectful, one of the few clients I miss.

"My sex life is so bad, my G-spot has been declared a historical landmark."

~ Joan Rivers.

12. Worst Sex, Best Sex

The worst sex I had was with a client in his mid-80s who'd book me as an escort. I used to go to his council flat which was really disgusting. He was blind and would exercise on an *exercycle* in his undies. He stank, his flat stank and was a mess and he'd just slobber all over me and eat me out. But he would come quite quickly and I was relieved because the booking would end and I could get out of there with my fee.

I really didn't like that client so I stopped taking the bookings and other girls had to service him. Paid Love is what it is; you have to be professional but you always have choices and I just found it too disgusting. I have some self-respect. It wasn't about his age or the fact that he was blind (I did plenty of disabled bookings and we had a wheelchair room, that is, a room wide enough to accommodate a wheelchair and sexual activity with a bigger open shower and the queen size bed) it's just that he was really unhygienic and his flat was depressing. Why would you invite an attractive woman to your flat to have sex with her and not clean up beforehand? And not have yourself and the environment smelling nice? How much is a bottle of cologne!? It was just about him getting his rocks off and you're just there as a means to an end. So I didn't feel like I owed him much and removed myself from his radar.

A 'Jake the Muss' character came in, a member of a gang. That booking was one of my worst experiences working in prostitution. I was the only girl allowed to go through with him. He had thick black dreadlocks that hung over his face. Stocky and powerful, clearly he'd planned it. As I emerged from the shower, naked and vulnerable, I was grabbed, lifted to waist height and thrown roughly across the room into the wall. He advanced like a silverback gorilla. I curled into a foetal ball and began to laugh uncontrollably. It probably saved my life.

The manager paired me with him because of his look, and his attitude. He hardly spoke, just grunted. After he paid the standard rate with the manager, she said to me,

> "You don't have to go with him; but I'm not giving him to any of the other girls. You have the maturity to handle him."

I felt nervous. He was a short stocky guy and looked really strong. I felt I could handle him and being money driven, accepted the challenge and I led him to the room.

He jumped in to the shower first, clearly he'd done this before at other clubs. I followed, showered, and as I came out and reached for the towel on the hook, that's when he grabbed me. It was completely unexpected, caught me off balance. It was completely animalistic and lustful. In hindsight, I think he was trying to be intimidating, acting out an insecure over each and masking a persona to hide anxiety, fear and hurt.

I laughed, because that's what I do when I'm really nervous or scared. But it seemed to disarm him. I'd fallen onto the bed off the wall and he came over, knelt on the bed, spread my legs apart, and just stared at me. Probably trying to work me out.

He leaned down and kissed me gently on the lips and was a 'pussy cat' after that, really tender. I went along with that, to make the booking work. I don't remember him speaking once. The sex was over pretty quickly, standard intercourse, he came, after that he was done. He got dressed and left. I cleaned up thankful it was over. The manager and some of the girls came in to check on me.

They asked how it went and was I ok? I was, but relieved that it went ok and I'd got this one done. I got my money. I didn't feel anything to be honest; you don't with people like that. We never saw him again.

The best sex I ever had was with one of my cop clients who was really good. Big cock, not huge, really easy to talk to and have sex with. He was a good fit really (I mean literally). I first met him in the lounge. He wanted two girls but I didn't like him because he was loud and a bit obnoxious. Two young girls went up to him and he booked them.

About 15 minutes later one of the girls buzzed the manager, and said he wanted another girl, to replace them both, someone that could keep up with his sexual demands. The manager sent me upstairs and I remember thinking *"Oh, this guy!"*

It was a bit awkward, because he wasn't getting what he wanted from the two young girls (not an uncommon problem I have to say). I came in. One of the girls pulled me aside, and said *"He's really hard work, he wants to bang really hard."* He was too full on for them.

I thought, *"Oh shit."* But because of his cocky arrogant attitude, I thought, *"bring it on, I'll sort him out."* I looked at him and felt I could handle him.

The two girls left and I took over the booking. The guy was a maniac, it was any which way, and heaps of fun, and he fucked my brains out, and I fucked his brains out. It was a challenge, and he was trying to break me down with his cock, and I was rising to the challenge. We actually became friendly.

We must have banged me for about three hours. Obviously he wasn't coming. I don't know what he was on, but I remember this client and this sex because it was so good. Long. I was up for it. I got really satisfied and enjoyed his focus and physical attention on me. He was actually quite funny. A bit of a joker, which I didn't see at first.

I had him a few times in The Club, then I went back to his house as a private. We had sex in his bed and he came, like normal. It was lovely and normal, unlike the three-hour banging under the influence of some drug at The Club.

My second big regular client was six foot four; had a really nice body and the sex was really great. Those kinds of clients helped you get through the dross bookings. If you had the right clients, it could be quite glamorous. I had plenty of nice looking professional clients, who'd take me out to nice restaurants, back to a glamorous hotel, the sex could be good, great or just ok, and overall you felt good, appreciated, wanted, glamorous. The bookings on the yachts were glamorous. You still had to strip off all your clothes and fuck in front of everyone but other than that, it could be alright. Good nights and bad nights.

My third regular big client was an IT guy. He would come in regularly and book lots of girls to sit with him in the lounge. He never had or wanted sex. Instead, he liked to talk about his work and also politics.

Most of his conversation with me would go in one ear and out the other. He was a strange character somewhat eccentric, but I learned he had a very difficult upbringing. He was very intelligent, almost on the spectrum. I tolerated his idiosyncrasies but he would book for hours and I actually quite liked him.

Being in the lounge, other guys thought we were available, but we weren't. Other clients didn't understand that we'd already been booked, to sit there and chat in the lounge, instead of being taken to a room for sex. He just liked the attention and it was a super easy booking with drinks thrown in.

One celebrity sportsman came in. He was gorgeous, muscles bulging, tall, athletic, beautiful ruddy complexion. I was so pleased when he booked me. I took him to the room. He was actually very shy and quite quiet and –like many gigs– sort of covered himself up while showering with me in the cubicle with him. Men in brothels can be quite coy. We showered, lay together on the bed, and OH MY GOSH, the smallest penis in the universe!! I mean, tiny. Literally the size of my little finger on a huge attractive masculine body. Probably the side effect of steroids.

All I could do was massage it with two fingers, to try and get him erect and to come. He did get erect, but I sat on him cowboy, one of those *"Is it in yet?"* moments. I umm-ed and ahh-ed a lot, sort of lap danced him. I never knew if he came or not.

Good sex was mostly with younger guys who were really good looking and had large cocks. Because the vagina stretches, you get more pleasure from larger cocks. But if you're in a relationship, you don't want a large cock, because it can hurt too much. Some women are married to guys with large cocks and they love it, but that's because they are probably physically compatible. The young guys would just get on with it. When you're a prostitute, you're not really looking to enjoy the sex, you're just going through the motions, collecting the money. Like eating ice cream all day as quality control in a factory. You get sick of ice cream. Which means it's time to get out. You don't want sex in your private life, so it can really damage personal relationships.

It can take a while to get re-balanced and back to normal, sexually and emotionally. My 'balance' was off. What I mean is, I had lots of sex at work but hardly any at home. (Some girls are actually entirely celibate outside work). I was 'cold' at work, turned off emotionally, tuned-out. That is what I had to do afterward, re-balance; get turned on again in a normal relationship, tune in to my partner sexually and get normal emotions back (love, affection, caring, desire).

With good sex, it always helps if clients are friendly and funny and you have a good conversation; you're in there for a whole hour or longer, and that helps the time pass. It doesn't matter if they talk dirty or are quiet, you just go with the flow, as part of the job. It's actually "good sex" if it's over and done with fairly quickly. You can't go with guy after guy and enjoy it. You get exhausted.

I had one young client who could't even get to first base. He'd come in the shower before we even got on the bed. Premature ejaculation. The best sex ever! Then I'd just chat to him. Every time he came in, he'd book me, and try really hard not to come in the shower. But he did every time. I felt really sorry for him. He was a really good looking boy (wouldn't have had any trouble finding a girlfriend; maybe that's why he came in, to try and sort that out, his premature ejaculating; get more used to sex and learn to manage himself). I'd give him a massage and chat and then his hour would be up.

One of my favorite clients was a retired military man, an older guy who'd seen action in places like Iraq and Afghanistan, although he would't discuss it much. I knew he'd been in Special Services of some type. He'd been on some pretty gnarly ops. He'd come in and book me for two hours and just whole-body massage me the whole time, front and back, a little bit of external light fingering, but nothing penetrative. I'd lay there naked and get paid for being massaged. It was heaven. He'd bring in some beautiful textiles, like silk, feathers, sheets, a towel and gently run them across my body. It is very sensual and that seemed to be his thing; we never had sex. I'd say, *"Well, do you want me to massage you?"* He never wanted that and seemed to like pleasuring me and seeing me enjoy what he was doing.

He'd shower as required and wrap a towel around his waste, but never wanted a blow job. He booked me several times. Perhaps he had war wounds and was embarrassed to be touched himself or was working through some trauma from his operations; assuaging guilt or trying to be nice to women after all the female suffering he'd seen. Maybe some of it he was involved in, so this was a way to turn that psychology around for him. Whatever it was, a perfect client and he was such a sweetie.

Really bad sex was the guys who thrust really slowly and couldn't come and no emotional connection. They'd thrust really slowly for a very long time, it was tedious, I actually fell asleep once with a client in me. He woke me up, and said,

"Are you asleep?"

"No, I'm just enjoying it, closed my eyes to feel it more."

You get good at lying while laying.

You'd be laying there on your back and he's banging away really slowly and there's no train in the tunnel. He just pulls out and we're done. Deflation (literally). It's bad because it's boring as hell, and your vagina dries up so you have to keep lubricating all the time. He's groaning and sighing, so you have to go all fake on him for 40 minutes and that's exhausting. You can't just lay there and say or do nothing. You have to move and sigh as if it's the best sex you've ever had, throw in some dirty talk, and try and pad out what is tediously dull.

I had a few dwarf clients, "Little People" as they prefer to be called. The ones I had, for some reason, had chips on their shoulders. Angry. They were rough and had bad attitude as if they were trying to exorcise something out of their psyche "small man syndrome" (applies to non-dwarfs too just as much). He banged on all the time about how badly off he was, then treated me like shit and banged me. He never saw the irony.

Having sex with a dwarf is a bit weird, his head is on your stomach. I felt they were the same, like any other man, except they were shorter. And let's face it, even a tall man goes down there, so it's like he's a dwarf anyway. Their cocks are shorter, like their digit's, so that myth about dwarfs having massive relative cocks, is untrue. Maybe for some, but not with the ones I had. One was especially Grumpy (hah hah) and so much so, I used to avoid him when he came in to the lounge. I'd stay away or tell the manager I was with another client, so I didn't get booked preferentially every time he came in. Same with any other regular client you want to avoid, you just leave the lounge.

Some ethnic men liked to bite and were very rough. You had to tell them off and stop that. I once had my nipples badly bitten and my clit and it really hurts. They don't get carried away, they seem to do it on purpose. It's a power play. They liked to be dominant in the bedroom. Luckily enough most of them were small enough to toss against the wall if they played up, and once that happens, well the sex is off because the tone has altered. Girls have that power. Unless she's willing, no client is going to get any action from a girl who's pissed off because of their behavior. If they tried anything, despite paying, it would be rape.

It's a difficult one If someone has booked you and you go in to a room, it's clear you are consenting to sex. Money has exchanged. There's a procedure to go through, protocol. Guys must always have a shower first. So, if they come in, thrown you on the bed and jump on top of you, or try to give you anal when you not offered that and you're saying 'No! No!" and he's persisting, well, that is rape. It makes no difference if you're in a brothel.

Reluctant prostitute Jill Brenneman from New Hampshire, who before she began working in the sex trade to pay medical debts, was tortured and brutalized as an abducted imprisoned sex slave by a narcissist kidnapper who pimped her out to sadistic clients, went on to co-found a sex workers outreach project and *Sex Workers Without Borders*. Jill says,

> "As a sex worker I agree to do certain things. Anything I am forced to do outside [of] that is rape, plain and simple. Clients know that sex workers can't go to police or even seek medical help. Many of them become violent because they know they can get away with it." [9]

---

[9] "A former sex slave's terrifying ordeal: "As soon as he put the blindfold on, I knew something was wrong," *Salon health newsletter*, Tessie Castillo, 4 May 2015.

"I don't really think myself tat sex work is necessarily more demeaning than other kinds of demeaning work."

~ Alix Kates Shulman.

13. The Daily Grind(ing)

There *are* sexual differences between cultures, but I don't want to go in to that. Some cultures are rude, pushy, and they try to push the boundaries. Early on I learned I had to clarify my services. For example, a guy came on my face. It was disgusting. I'm not really in to that, but if he'd asked first, maybe I would have allowed it, but more likely said no. But another guy might just do it without asking. That's contemptuous. Just because you're paying doesn't make your girl a commodity you can disrespect or abuse. It's a service. Like treating waitresses kindly, even if they stuff up.

In this game, you're giving them your body. They should be respectful and if they aren't or are self-centered, then they're just assholes which I won't be servicing.

There's a light in the lounge that comes on, which means someone is at the discrete backdoor entrance, the one Michelle and I came in on our first visit. One of the girls is expected to go and see. There's a camera. It's a good way to get a booking because you're the first girl to meet the client.

I let in a client who said he was a top international yachtsmen, so I popped him into one of the rooms and buzzed the manager as he said he had a pre-arranged booking. I chatted to him a bit while he sat on his own, until the manager came in to get his booking sorted. But he said, "Actually. I'd like to go with Jasmin now."

We had nice sex, he came pretty quickly, and then he asked if I'd like to have a back rub. In those days, my lower back muscles were very strong and tight. He massaged me for 30 minutes or more. It was really nice. That was really rare to get that from a client after sex.

Usually once they were done, and had come, you're discarded. Massaging me was an acknowledgement of my humanity as a person and I have always remembered that. It was even nicer because he was so handsome.

A really high percentage of men have small cocks and can't get a hard on. It's perhaps why such a high percentage of those kinds of men are in brothels, so perhaps it's a skewed measure. We saw more men with small cocks than was perhaps normal. Least, that was my experience. There's nothing worse than giving a soft cock a hand or blow job. It's awful. That's why all women like hard cock. And I came to appreciate that much more after years in the game. I liked it because it made work easier, but over time I came to like it much more in my own mind and sexually. It's attractive, It's really masculine and excites your femininity.

A hard cock shows a woman that a man is turned on by her and that makes you feel good. If he doesn't get hard, many women take that personally, because women take everything personally. You might in your private life, but at work, less so. Nevertheless, hard cock is the currency of the business.

My first threesome with two men (which is different from a bi-girl booking) was with two young men. One was really drunk. I was probably really drunk too. It didn't go very well, because we were all too drunk. They couldn't get hard, so they couldn't penetrate, they just rubbed up against me and it becomes drunken petting. Ok by me, having two men, one maybe kissing my face the other giving me oral sex. It's very flattering and having that much male energy focussed on you as one woman is very erotic and stirs you up as a woman.

If two guys are really hard and doing you together, that's very satisfying, but no more than two drunk guys petting you together. It's not about the sex, which men seem to fixate on. For women it's about the attention, the touch, that you are attractive to the two males and garnering their focus and attention. The allure. Women want to attract and be attractive.

Shortly after that I had my first foursome, a really well known sportsmen, his mate, me and Tania. We went in to a room after a big game and after-match parties. It was at The Club. It was a bit of an orgy, the mate was vaginally fisting me and I remember I squirted. It was a long booking, it was fun, we were all very drunk. It was relaxed, lots of joking and chit chat and it was never too intense on the sex. The sportsman became a regular client after that, but usually just one-on-one.

Then I had a six-some, four girls and two guys. But one of the guys wanted me one-on-one, which I did. He just wanted his balls sucked. He wanked off and came in about ten minutes, and the booking was done.

A professor came in to The Club and took me to a swanky hotel. I was dined and fucked in the hotel room and then went back to The Club and got another dinner date with several other girls at an ethnic restaurant. After two big restaurant meals of rich food, I was really full. You can imagine I didn't want sex missionary style, some big guy pressing down on my stomach. So I went doggy-style, which a lot of guys liked anyway.

A wealthy city businessman used to book me reasonably regularly. He'd usually book me but sometimes another girl and we'd go back to his city house which was really opulent; a beautiful swimming pool, and really well appointed. We'd dance in the lounge, he'd always offer us dope, which I smoke occasionally but usually it made me fall asleep. So I didn't do a lot of dope, but he liked it and the other girls smoked and we drank heaps of wine. I went upstairs to have sex with them but the dope made me fall asleep on the bed, a great way to do a four hour booking! He didn't seem to mind because he was probably busy with the other girls and I was just there as eye candy, naked and asleep on the bed.

He did eventually wake me up after he'd finished with the other girls, saying,

> "I really like you Jasmine, but not enough to pay you to sleep in my house!"

I got up, got dressed and we all left. Still got my four hour fee, though. But you can't push that, you won't get repeat clients.

Falling asleep was common. Sometimes there'd be half a dozen of us, all asleep together like sardines in the big room (used for group sex). We seemed to all 'hit the wall' about 4am on night shift.

One of the other managers was Irish, a really fat blonde chick who liked to flirt with clients because she thought that was the way to get bookings for the other girls. But it was more than likely a turn-off, or maybe it frightened them into bookings with the younger chicks! But she was lovely and I really liked her and her accent was cool which the clients also often liked. It made the establishment feel like it was legit or European or something.

One time she was flirting with some clients trying to get bookings and the client said *"show us your tits"* so she took them into a back room and flipped her top and got paid for the flash. A quick fee for the manager which she's not really supposed to do, but hey, there's lots of free money slushing around at clubs and you just went with the flow. Good for her.

Chloe was another manager, a bit corrupt. She tended to take bookings for girls that would give her a 'kick-back' to give them preference. She was on the take on the side on top of her manager salary which is a real 'no no'. I had a big falling out with her, which went on for months. Eventually she left. Apparently I 'broke her' according to the other girls. I never liked that kind of crap. It undermined the business, undermined our relationships with clients. Maybe it was a power play by her.

I liked good managers who were really strict but fair, and I liked the stability of that. The Club could be chaotic at times with drunk guys, drunk girls, drugs, all sorts of unsociable characters, so you needed a strong anchor. I liked it because everything tended to run smoothly. A lot of these managers who are good at managing people last a long time and made a career of it. They were real assets to the clubs because they got to know the clients, heard what was going on in the scene, could sniff out dodginess. They got to know everyone, and got good at matching girls with appropriate clients so the bookings went well. All-in-all they were the glue that held the clubs together and were the perfect conduit between the owners and the girls and the clients. The roster manager is a key to a successful club and a successful business.

The security guys at The Club were a mixed range of men and sometimes women: some big beefy gorillas, others just ordinary guys who knew how to handle themselves.

The security staff were amazing when I first joined. They'd escort me to my car late at night, drive me out to a location, sometimes wait, come pick me up. Often they were outside the door listening, if a client looked dodgy, and were straight in if there was any banging or sounds of trouble. But over time that changed. Security was cut back, staff who were not as committed to us were hired, who didn't seem to care, it wasn't the same. They were usually big men and were under strict instructions never to come on to the girls, to keep it professional, they were people we needed to trust. Some didn't follow that rule, and got fired. It was a bit of a case of some of the girls coming on to them, as some of them were quite good looking. So, it was sad if they lost their job not being able to resist some of the girls advances.

Some of the guys got on with the girls, others didn't. Their additional work involved doing all the laundry, re-stocking the bar and chauffeur escorts to jobs and then take payment. They'd also check escort job premises for cameras and anything dodgy like that.

If we were out on escort and had an 'off' feeling or just simply didn't want to go through with the booking for whatever reason, we had a code. We'd call up security and say,

> *"I'm out of condoms, there is more in the car could you bring some up?"*

And that was code we wanted them to come and get us and cancel the booking because we felt unsafe or were in danger.

A lot of clients look like famous people or had similar names so we had lots of nicknames for them. Even our names were fake. There was a guy called Neil so we called him "Armstrong."

Another guy looked like President Bill Clinton so we called him "Bill" or "the President." The manager would say, *"Hey, the president's coming in, Jasmin!"*

We had a girl called Lilly who was really tall, so we called her Everest. She was an addict and started to act up under the influence, getting abusive and 'out of it.' So she got sacked.

Another regular client came in, Tony, and he'd won lots of money on the horses. These guys were foolish, because they blew the whole lot on prostitutes. He won enough on the horses for a house deposit but they were just drinking, doing drugs and sexing it away. And of course they'd boast, and gangsters would hear about it and stand them over and take it or the drugs they'd bought with it. Everybody was ripping everybody off all the time. One of the girls who flatted with me at one time, had accumulated several thousand dollars for a trip to Europe. For some stupid reason she told her landlord, and sure enough, all her cash went missing. Of course she couldn't prove anything, but she knew who took it. I told her at the time, *"Just stop paying rent!"*

A young guy who came in to The Club got an inheritance from his aunt. He came in every night booking the same two girls for hours and hours until all his aunt's money was gone. Disrespectful, contemptuous and stupid! That aunt may have saved for years to accumulate that money which he blew on sexual gratification in a few weeks.

Another man, late thirties, one of the most beautiful men I'd ever seen (he looked a bit like Joaquin Phoenix) booked me and occasionally other girls, all on an inheritance from his father. He'd come in every couple of weeks for years until the money ran out.

I had a really funny client who would book me weekly. Sometimes just me, other times as a threesome. He would always book a single hour but usually then extend to six or seven hours.

He took a long time to come, but when he did, he would habitually rapidly get dressed without showering, and swiftly leave the room, swearing and cursing down the corridor, that he'd spent too much money, felt ripped off, and would never come back again! Until next Friday night and we went through the whole charade all over again. That lasted over five years; he was one of my 'bread and butter' clients.

On one occasion he was booking another girl because I was on another booking. As I came in to the lounge, he saw me as he was about to pay, and cancelled his booking telling the manager he wanted to book me instead. I felt bad for the other girl.

The manager gave me the evils, and pulled me aside, saying *"Amanda hasn't had a booking yet, maybe you should let this client go with her."* But it wasn't up to me, my regular client wanted to switch, and he had me every Friday night. So, no, I wasn't about to give him up just because Amanda hadn't had a booking yet. He was my client. The girl was pissed off with me, but she got over it.

The Club was always 'swings and roundabouts,' and there were plenty of occasions when I missed out. That girl got heaps of clients anyway, as she was a P addict and supplied drugs to her bookings.

I had a few cross dresser clients. But sex with them was always conventional, like with a man. It didn't really turn me off it was more amusing than anything else. They obviously have a female gig going on in their head, but generally still liked getting 'head.' They were dressing to accommodate a mind thing, but in The Club they wanted sex like any other man. They'd take me as a woman but they'd bang me as a man. They were really like any other client. The way they dress and behave was kind of amusing and entertaining and made the long 12 hour shifts a bit more fun.

Edward was a politician. He was a liar and a loudmouth and was quite unpopular with the girls. I went with him once. He was really rough in the room and after that he got really clingy and wanted me to go out with him and take me out; he became a problematic client and I passed him on to someone else. I don't know if he made public office or not, I never heard from him much after that.

I had a few lawyers, maybe I was the sort of girl they liked. As well as Andy, I also had a few politicians, although they tended not to disclose that, and I wasn't really into politics so I wouldn't have known if they were or not but some of the girls commented. Of course we never disclose who they were because that's very damaging to our industry and it affects our income. It's also very destructive for them, and that's their call not ours. You don't want to mess with people's lives like assholes do. We were literally doing enough assholes as it was!

I had an older gentleman as a regular client and I'm sure he was using *viagra* because he'd always be massively hard whenever he came in and he fucked really hard. A lot of guys lacked confidence and were afraid of being shamed in front of the girls. They felt they had to perform and be hard, so they'd fire up on *viagra* before coming in. It takes about half an hour to take effect and only actually works if there is desire. If you're not full of desire, then it won't work, and contrary to common misconception, you can 'go back down' on *viagra*. It simply engorges the penis, assists blood flow, but you still have to get horny. Some men would be erect for 24 hours and in agony and couldn't come down and had to go to hospital.

Sunny was a blonde Australian surfer guy who fancied himself. He thought he was Casanova, but actually was boring as hell and a bit bizarre. The sex was really bad and he fucked really slowly. On one occasion he pulled his condom off and fucked me from behind without his condom on. This is often a risk because you're so well lubricated and if he's doing you from behind you can't see. If he's slow, he can just whip it off and carry on and you wouldn't notice. You can pick up AIDS or an STD. I really hate guys like that who are disrespectful and contemptuous of you as a person and I could've had them fined. It's really bad when they do that. They put their moment of gratification (skin on skin) ahead of your entire life or health. I was fuming and really told him off and refused to go through with him after this incident.

Some women are exhibitionists, they like to be watched or to parade. Others are more demure. I was never an exhibitionist; it was never a fantasy for me, to have a whole bunch of men or women look at me, watch me having sex, but I didn't mind it, if the money was right. I'd do it, but it wasn't really my thing; and if I was doing swinging gigs, I'd usually be so plastered it didn't matter.

I was in the shower with a client at the beginning of a booking and he was really drunk. He slipped over in the shower and had his hands around my neck and pulled me down with him. I cracked two ribs on the edge of the shower but carried on working (I also once worked with a broken toe). It was a painful three weeks.

I was so tired one night that I ironed my ear with my iron. My ear was crusty and flaky for a week, like a cornflake.

Some of my quietist nights ever was when I only had a single booking. I was really pissed off. It's a long time to work 12 hours with one hour of sex. Us girls would often fall asleep after 4am in the lounge on nightshift, or be on our phones just waiting around for clients to come in. Managers would come and if it was quiet, give us exercises to do, like at a gym, to wake us up, keep us focussed.

With all the kissing, I actually got gingivitis three or four times because there's an exchange of bacteria. There are actually over 500-600 different species of bacteria in your mouth, way more than your anus.

I went on really strong antibiotics to clear it up, because once you have gingivitis, you are susceptible to that bacterial infection ever after that.

It can take a while to clear up, and you have to avoid kissing while you're working. Gingivitis cost me a fortune in treatments so there are always downsides to this game and costs, like with any business or trade.

Gingivitis is really nasty. Your gums sting and your mouth stinks because of the bacteria. They also bleed and it's quite painful. You can just eat a piece of bread and your gums bleed. It cost me thousands in treatments over several sessions. At one stage I had to have all my gums cut and lifted and all the bacteria scraped out to get my gums to come right. It's a real pain to get it and I had it three or four times while I was working.

Having been an athlete I was pretty fastidious about my personal health and I always had good dental health. But if you're kissing guys with really bad dental health or oral hygiene you pick up bacteria. When I went to my dentist I did explain that I was a hooker and I was kissing a lot of men. That helped her to understand what my problem was rather then that I just had bad dental hygiene. She was sympathetic and helped me out a lot to overcome infections I picked up with work. That's why a lot of girls won't kiss on bookings because they just don't want to get their mouth infected and why some won't do oral.

You do oral sex with a condom anyway but you can actually pick up an infection from the latex rubber if you're sensitive to it. My gums would often tingle unpleasantly after sucking on a condom. There are 'fish hooks' everywhere in the game.

When you're on the oral antibiotics you can't drink alcohol and I had gingivitis during my birthday so that sucked. I couldn't have any celebratory drinks for my birthday because some dirty client with really bad oral health gave me some hideous bacterial infection. A few times I forgot to not drink and ended up vomiting.

When I first started I was really surprised when guys booked me continually but didn't have sex. I had one regular client book me five different times and we never had sex (what's wrong with men!?). But as the years progressed, I got used to this. It's quite common. Often men don't want to have sex, they just want the company.

Sometimes they were ashamed and loved their wives but weren't getting what they wanted or needed from their partner. They didn't want to have sex with a prostitute but they'd come into the brothel and participate by chatting to an attractive young woman with the suggestion or possibility of sex and that was usually enough for them. And they'd go back to their wives having not 'cheated' on them (not had sex) but had "been to a brothel;" they just wanted intimacy. They might put their hand on your knee or put their hand around you, buy you drinks, and chat, often about their spouse and partner.

One night we were really busy and it was absolute chaos in The Club; men everywhere and three men tried to book me at the same time. One was from Laos. He was a real hunk with a beautiful complexion. You'd usually go with the guy who talked to you first or the longest, but if you had a choice, the one who is really good looking. Obviously I want sex with good-looking guys. The other two lost out.

There were two Barflies who took girls out for dinner all the time. One of them had a reputation for being really rough so girls wouldn't go with him, so he'd just take us all out for dinner which suited us fine.

Valentines Day was, ironically, terrible at The Club. Guys would take their girlfriends or wives out for dinner and we'd be abandoned. It was usually a very quiet night. I did have a few nights where there were no clients at all. Zero pay. We'd all get pissed off but that's just the game. Staying up all night, going to the trouble of getting all that makeup on, and no clients. But you offset the disappointment with the fact you'd already made a lot of money earlier in the week.

One night to just fill-in, I massaged the manager's shoulders. A 5am-er came in and booked me because he saw me massaging. He was done in half an hour and out.

When the client's hour had ten minutes to go, the manager would buzz the room and say "ten minutes!" as clients were waiting to use the room. Autumn was in a room and there was no reply. They waited ten minutes. The manager went up and knocked on the door, still no reply. One of the other girls had noticed on the camera that the client had left early. The Club had to kick the door in because they couldn't find the key. Autumn was on the bed unconscious which freaked everyone out.

She'd been GHB-drugged and probably raped. [10] The client had been out of jail just a week. She was carted off to the hospital by paramedics.

Occasionally The Club would go on a spate of firing people to clean out girls who weren't attracting bookings and to reduce costs. Cutting staff. You can't have too many girls on a shift, because the place wasn't that big. So the girls who were there, had to be pulling bookings so the establishment got paid.

In The Club, Friday or Saturday night we'd have 20-25 girls feeding 15 rooms. One girl got fired for texting on a quiet night. Just an excuse to get rid of her, really.

We'd have girls coming in from other cities, flat broke, living day-to-day in a hostel. It would take time for them

---

[10] "GHB" Gamma Hydroxybutyric Acid is a generic coverall for a variety of drugs like LSD, ecstasy and ketamine used in date rape drugs cases. It incapacitates girls and guys screw them *non compos mentis*. [Editor].

to break in to the regular clientele. So, it's not all fists full of dollars for fisting. You have to put in the time, build the rapport and get repeat clients, to make it work. But these girls often only stayed a month or two, so they never got promoted to clients, because management knew they would go again. And they did. Those girls were always looking for the easy money and missed out on it because they failed to build any regular client base. Lazy.

We used to dread the big sports fixtures as lots of clients would come in after the games, really drunk and 'laddish.'

One night I was so tired, I turned up to work with two different black heels on. There was always a serious lack of sleep in this game, one of the reasons I eventually got out. Alcohol and drugs doesn't help. But selling your body takes a definite toll and like other workers who use their bodies directly, it is extremely tiring.

A car dealer booked me, after a good night of seven bookings (six were escort with a repeat regular client). The dealer banged me so hard I had a sore clitoris. In that circumstance, you just keep going.

A regular client booked me for a private and I did a deal with him on the cheap. He was such a good client I went with it. When I got there he said he didn't have any cash but would pay it into my account. I let it go – something I would NEVER do (you don't sell your body to a guy on credit)– but I knew this client really well. We'd talked about dating for a while, but he was a heavy drinker. I trusted him enough to give him the night on promised credit and at a much lower rate, because he'd blown so many thousands on me previously.

We slept together, but it was disconcerting to find naked pictures of myself on his phone, which he showed me. I had been asleep that previous night and he'd snapped me while on the escort. He deleted them in front of me. That's a big 'no no,' I don't want be sold online so someone else makes money or family to see me online naked or sold as product to porn sites.

The following Tuesday that client finally paid up, a relief. If he hadn't I would have sent Andrew my buff boyfriend around to sort him out. He might have hurt that client; I was ok about that because a deal is a deal. I'm a stickler for the protocol and the arrangements, especially as I am the product. Once you start sliding on that kind of thing, you get owned and exploited.

I'd sometimes go see a Reiki masseuse which seemed to help. I got home one night from a Reiki session and received an email, that my dad had died. He was in his eighties and lived in another country. I was devastated, and obviously didn't work that night. I loved my dad, we were close. He didn't know I was a prostitute. I'd never told him, because he would've been disappointed with me. I was ok with that, there are just some things you can't tell some people. It was really sad as Dad had already been dead three days so I wasn't at the service.

I only got ripped off once in my years in the game. Girls get ripped off a lot. Everyone is ripping off everyone else. There's lots of cash slushing about; girls have wads in their bags. They get drunk. Clients take their bags. Girls rob clients wallets while they're passed out or in the shower.

A client from out of town had come in to The Club and booked Amy one day and me the next, big bookings. So he had cash. That cost him a lot. The next week he had me and told me he'd like to have a private, so I gave him my work number. Often you had a separate cell phone for work contacts and only used it while working, to keep your non-work life separate.

He rang about a week later and I persuaded him to do a threesome with Michelle and agreed to a price each. She and I went to a motel where he was staying. He made us dinner in the unit but couldn't provide the cash. I said just pay it directly into our account. For whatever reason, he wasn't able to, but said he'd go up to the ATM machine in the morning. He had a dog with him, so we felt he wasn't going anywhere, so we had sex and slept together.

In the morning he was up early, something about having to "open up" his workshop. While we slept or were drowsy, he left, came back and gave us $100, as a down payment but said he had to go to work. The next few hours he played us, excuses and reasons why he couldn't pay up immediately. We also noticed he'd taken all his stuff. As he was leaving I said to leave the doggy here, we'll look after him, but he took it anyway, saying she always like to come with him in to work.

Eventually, he persuaded us to come up to a suburb and meet us at a bank where he would pay us. We foolishly drove there, probably the opposite direction to where he was heading. Of course, he never turned up. I kicked myself afterward that I never got his license plate number. If I'd got that as he pulled out of the carpark, we would've had him. He was probably using a throw-away phone so trying to get a trace from that would've been a dead end. With cop contacts (several were clients) it was easy to trace someone like that, from their license plate number.

We went back to the motel and tried to get the guy's name and address from the registry book. The Asian manager was having none of it, so I just grabbed her book. He'd just scribbled a name and signed it, no other particulars. Probably paid cash.

When I got home, I told my boyfriend. He was furious and took some heavies back to the motel to try and find a contact for the guy. But came away with nothing.

Michelle and I were really pissed off. It's a form of theft. We'd provided a service, there was a contract, and an agreed price. If we'd gone to the police, it would have been theft, but we were on a "private" so The Club couldn't find out. He probably knew that. So, he got both of us for free, all night, and all we got was $50 each. He'd probably done it before.

But a guy like that will always get his comeuppance. You can't go around ripping off hookers like that; they have too many men in their lives that feel connected to them (that they've fucked) and who are protective of "their girl." That is a very dangerous and foolish game to play for the sake of some free sex. Or maybe it was a controlling thing, see if he could manipulate and control and get it all for nothing. A game of 'cat and mouse.' Some people get off on that adrenalin.

What I did learn was, NEVER accept credit. Always get the payment upfront. That's why the clubs work, because they run a tight ship and girls always get paid. Out on privates, it's the 'Wild West.'

'Jumping on' was a way of getting more hours on another shift to make more money or make ends meet if work was slow. Most clubs are pretty loose but the club I worked with was rather strict and had a roster and you had to keep to it. But, I might come in at 5 o'clock on an evening when I started at 6pm and try and get booked for an hour to make some extra money. One time I came in and a client booked me at 5pm but the manager noticed and came and grabbed me and pulled me off the booking and told me off because I didn't start till 6pm.

The reason for this is that clubs don't want too many girls on the floor on a quiet night. It draws clients away from the girls who are rostered on; and if they get slim pickings, they might leave and go elsewhere. This is what happened with me, I basically took a client off one of the day roster girls, to make extra money before my night shift. The client had been a day client and had got a bit sick of the regular girls. He saw me come in, a 'new' girl and booked me. After I was pulled off the booking he actually left so the day girl didn't get the job anyway.

I can see the point but you need to have some flexibility with rosters. Anyway, the day girls used to stay on after their shifts and eat into our night schedules taking clients away from us, so it was always 'swings and roundabouts.'

A lot of cops came in as clients. Three cops came in once and booked a room for six: me, Rose and Carla. The cops didn't have sex with us, they just sat watching porn on their laptops the whole time and snorting cocaine (the recreational drug of choice at the time). One snorted it off my thigh. They just wanted us to stand around naked or lie on the bed and masturbate while they watched their porn. We didn't have any sex at all.

Police work is tough like prostitution, so it wasn't surprising we saw a lot of cops coming in after shift or before shift out of uniform to get release and comfort and nurture, if they weren't getting it at home from their girlfriends or their wives. You've all seen those cop dramas about bad cops, taking drugs on the side, like *The Bad Lieutenant* (Nicolas Cage).

Some people are really down on this because they see it as corruption, perhaps it is. Maybe it compromises the police officers, certainly puts them in contact with vice, drug money, gangs and that can be a difficult symbiosis.

But I saw it for the humanity it was. These were hard-working guys who saw a lot of awful stuff and dealt with the absolute dross of life at the very sharp end and needed some human warmth, nurture, kindness and love to help them through. Unfortunately the three cops that booked us that night were all addicted to pornography. Maybe that's how they got their rocks off most of the time. Porn ruins sex and relationships, probably why their home life was no good, or because of it.

It distresses me seeing all these young men getting hooked on pornography and how it ruins their capacity to have meaningful adult relationships with young women or get married and have families. They live in this fantasy sex world that pornography presents to them. It ruins people. It's an absolute scourge on our society but we live in an open society and people are allowed to choose. But choices have consequences and we're 'reaping a whirlwind' for all that "freedom" we're so precious about espousing.

A loud ethnic man came in, insisting his friend be given a [racial slur]. This annoyed two pilots in the lounge and there was a 'Mexican stand-off.' It got heated and the ethnic man left. He'd caused trouble before and was eventually banned.

I had a few pilot clients and some of the girls really liked shagging pilots. It's a sexy profession and there is that Mile High Club (people who've shagged at 30,000 feet). But I was not happy because they would often go out with us and drink and I knew that they had flights in three or four hours. That's a real 'no no' with me. They shouldn't be drinking and then fly an airplane with 200 people in it. Not good, but I guess brain surgeons, police offices and politicians do it all the time so obviously pilots are going to do it too. All those long shifts and flying. It's a reality.

I did some bi-girls with a girl called Lyndal. She was really out there. Oh my gosh. She used to violate men; she would fart and piss on their face and give them golden showers even if they didn't ask (it was supposed to be a paid extra service). She seemed to really get off on it. Some clients were disgusted and one of them sent her out. He extended with me for another hour after she left. Maybe she was trying too hard or it was something she was into, that she couldn't suppress. I did golden showers, but only if requested and the client paid.

We started out as friends but in the end she hated me because I was taking a lot of her clients away. What was really happening was, she was turning them off during our bi's and I was hoovering up her disaffected clients. You have to remember, I had several clients and all they did was massage me with no sex. Not all guys who come to brothels want extreme fantasy sex. And offering that, doesn't always earn you repeat custom. You have to understand your clients and that is what a lot of the younger girls didn't understand.

I liked to work a sophisticated older woman vibe, intelligent, classy, and that attitude pulled me a lot of work over time, not the weird exotic empty-headed crap, just assuming what men wanted –extreme lustful exotic 'Wham-Bam-Thank-You-Mam.' They don't.

One of the managers came to me and said she'd been watching me on the floor.

" you have a really different style about you."

I wasn't sure what she meant.

"You stand your ground, in terms of self-respect. You're aloof; you give the guy an eyebrow, a wink, but stay where you are. It drives them crazy and they come over to you and you get the bookings."

I wasn't doing that deliberately, that's just how I am, but it seems to really turn guys on and my partner has since told me that it drives him crazy as well, so maybe that was just a natural talent I had.

A really tall businessman I'd had before came in to The Club. He looked like he was loaded with money and had an air about him. He was flocked by all the girls in the lounge, about 12 girls around him and he stood above them all like a poplar in a grass field. The guy kept yelling out,"*Jasmin! Jasmin*, rescue me!"

Y'see, he wanted a mature sophisticated woman he could talk to, not all the reef feeders from the lounge who just instantly gave head and took the money.

*"And all the vampires walkin' through the valley
Move west, down Ventura Boulevard
And all the bad boys are standin' in the shadows
And the good girls are home with broken hearts*

"And I'm free, I'm free fallin'."

~ *Tom Petty, Free Fallin'.*

14. Getting Out

As the years passed I became lazy in the job, losing interest in the work itself and dreaming of a better future; a life well away from The Club, the city, the nightlife, drunken parties, orgies, groveling slobbering men and meaningless sex.

I would instigate sexual conversation to stir up the client, get him excited, and invite him to do a threesome, then bring in other girls to the booking so I wouldn't have to 'perform.' Then I'd suggest to the client that we go for dinner or visit a strip club. It was an avoidance strategy, I suppose. The years and years of being 'hammered' physically and socially was taking its toll.

You get sick of drinking continually; clients are always giving you drinks. You take the alcohol because it's an important lubricant of the work, gets you through, helps the client relax and reduces inhibitions. The clients also think if they can get you drunk, they can do anything with you. It's up to the girl what goes on; some won't even kiss; or give a blow job; or take it up the ass. The drinks are also an important income stream.

We had a scam with the bar workers. If a client ordered a drink, say a Bacardi & Coke, we'd wink, and they'd just give us a coke, charge him the $10 for the Bacardi & Coke and we'd pocket the $10. All soft drinks were free to the girls.

There's also an emotional toll. You liked some clients but they were unavailable because they were married or if they were single, they wanted a relationship. But I was in one and couldn't mix work with pleasure. So, you were torn emotionally some of the time. Liking someone, but having to disengage all the time.

You have to adjust to each client; their personality, their body language, their sense of humor; their intelligence, fake interest at their dad jokes, their boasting, their insecure egos, their sense of awesomeness. It gets really tiring, emotionally draining. The highest amount of bookings I ever did, was 11 one hour booking over a 12-hour shift. That's 11 sexual encounters over 12 hours. Every man was different, had to be adjusted to. You can imagine the toll that takes.

One minute you're being fucked by Alan then next by Xavier and you have to adjust to each person. It's physically tiring. 11 bookings was probably over my limit.

If I'd been younger, I probably would have stayed, earned gazillions, invested it, and made an actual career. But because I came late to the game, I had to get out, and reconnect with myself and real life. Many of the girls took breaks of six months, a year; went off and had babies; but being younger, came back to the industry. It's much harder for older women. I started in my late forties.

My body was starting to get tired and sore. I gained weight from comfort eating and started to despise my body, my main asset for obtaining business. In my mind the clients became boring and tedious and nothing about the job excited me anymore. As well as losing my 'Jasmin mojo' at work, I was losing my mojo outside work as well. The work was leaking in to my real life, like those girls damaging themselves permanently by doing too much anal or fisting. I was starting to need psychological diapers.

I wanted the old me back, the real me, free of fake eyelashes, fake nails, botox, filler, hair straighteners and endlessly needing anal, vagina and leg waxing and endless hair appointments.

There's a lot of upkeep to sell your body. You're competing with younger girls all the time who are a conveyor belt of incoming new hires. And all you're doing is getting older. I became tired of it all. I got lazy.

About age 45 I started getting botox and filler to look younger as I wasn't happy with the way I looked. I stepped it up before I went to The Club because beginning required a whole refit: nails, hair, eyelashes etc., so it was natural to include some botox. Some spas will do everything, so it's easy to get a package deal.

The botox and filler gave me a frozen forehead, a 'trout pout' (pronounced lips) if you get too much and saggy eyelids. Your lips really hurt if you get too much filler (it dissipates over time). I was not happy but on the whole the results were good but costly. All-in-all, worth it.

Selling your body you have to spend money to make money.

When a girl left, if she'd been there a while and was one of the team, we'd usually have a send off. Some flowers, some drinks. When I announced I was going, they did that for me. But I had a really difficult week with the details of moving on (car, the house, other logistics) and getting stuff sorted, that I missed the party and didn't get a chance to say goodbye to people.

I'd rolled my dice. The game was over, my real life was about to begin again.

15. Epilogue

Several years on from leaving prostitution, I am now in the Greek Islands running a luxury boutique B&B, mainly for ex-pats. I met a lovely man online, who had no issues with my past, and we eventually got married. I've never been happier. After dating a few years, Liam got offered a management position in the Mediterranean managing luxury lodges and he asked me to go out with him. I didn't hesitate. We managed lodges for a few years and then started our own luxury B&B on one of the Greek Islands we especially loved. And we're still here in 2023.

Looking back, I have no regrets with the job itself, just my private life and how messed up it got with the people associated with the game. Would I do it all again? Yes, but I would've started at 20, saved like mad, and retired at 30. Hindsight is much wiser than reality.

I miss the girls and the camaraderie, a few of the clients, the good money to be had. But I'm over the luxury yachts, restaurants and parties which hold no allure for me anymore.

I haven't changed my thoughts about Paid Love and the role it plays in society, despite what people say. Without it, real needs, excesses and wants would spill out on to the streets, into domestic violence, rape, date-rape, pedophilia, incest, and longterm toxic relationships.

> *"Suppress prostitution, and capricious lusts will overthrow society." ~ Saint Augustine.*

For all it's bad reputation, what I and my friends did, helped a little bit to ease the difficult road humanity walks through the 21st century, especially men estranged from their girlfriends or wives.

Nawal El Saadawi, the Egyptian feminist writer, activist and physician, once said,

> *"Prostitution means sexual intercourse between a man and a woman aimed at satisfying the man's sexual and the woman's economic needs. It is obvious that sexual needs, even in a male dominated system, are not as urgent and important as economic needs which, if not*

satisfied, lead to disease and death. Yet society considers the woman's economic need as less vital than the man's sexual one."

She is so right.

It's why the 'Mayor of Casterbridge's wife' (no name herself in the story) allowed herself to be sold.

www.ingramcontent.com/pod-product-compliance
Lightning Source LLC
Chambersburg PA
CBHW042124100526
44587CB00026B/4169